'CARRY ME' BACK TO THE 70's'

A teenage fans perspective of following a band in the 1970's

Shelley James

© Copyright 2017 Shelley James

All rights reserved.
No part of this publication may be reproduced, stored in a retrieval system, or transmitted, in any form or by any means, electronic, mechanical, photocopying, recording or otherwise, without the prior written permission of the publisher.

British Library Cataloguing in Publication Data.
A catalogue record for this book is available from the British Library

ISBN 978 0 86071 735 5

A Commissioned Publication Printed by
MOORLEYS
Print, Design & Publishing
email: info@moorleys.co.uk • website: www.moorleys.co.uk

Acknowledgements

Ann French (nee – Paxton)
Alison Grey (nee – Morcom)
Carole Garrett (nee – Kirk)
Fran Norton
Gill Marrion (nee – Morris)
Grace Hargreaves
Helen Morris (nee – Maunders)
Jane Davies (nee – Blacker)
Julyet Harris
June Sims (nee – Keepence)
Lynne Brown (nee – Hudson)
Lynne Norton (nee – Tuvey)
Linda Stewart (nee – Beardsley)
Linda White
Lorraine Vickers-Bennett
Newton Wills
Pauline Vincent (nee – Tinker)
Teresa Summerton
Tony Prince
Vivien Lee
...and 'Flintlock'

Dedicated to the memory of my friend
Marie Cannon
We never screamed at a band together.
However we shared many smiley times on and off stage.

Contents

Chapter One
The Quirkes Of Being A Teenager!   1

Chapter Two
Stupenderific!   12

Chapter Three
Those Non-Event-Events!   24

Chapter Four
No Sex, No Drugs, Just Rock And Roll.   38

Chapter Five
Carrier Bags + Lip Gloss = Dagenham!   50

Chapter Six
No More Waiting or Anticipating.'77 Tour.   61

Chapter Seven
Carry Me – By Taxi – A Little Of The Way!   75

Chapter Eight
Redi, Shelley, Glow.   96

Chapter Nine
Bath In The Thames.   112

Chapter Ten
The Waiting Game.   123

Chapter Eleven
Packed Possibilities.   134

Chapter Twelve
When It Was Taken All Away.   148

Chapter Thirteen
Well FAN-cy That.   167

Chapter Fourteen
Songs, Trails and Puppy Dog Tales.   178

Chapter Fifteen
Carry On Screaming.   189

Foreword

"I think I was always a bigger fan of the fans than the actual artistes. I was president of The Elvis Presley, The Osmonds and the Flintlock Fan Clubs, all honours bestowed upon me by their fan clubs. I liked spotting boy bands who would appeal to my target listeners. The 7.30pm – 9pm show on Radio Luxembourg was the background sound for boys and girls getting to grips with their homework.

I think I first met Flintlock through the Pinnacle record label when I was invited onto a TV show they starred in. 'FAB208' magazine was just as interested in young bands as I was and so their full colour pictures started to attract an army of fans. We did a few photo sessions together for 'FAB208', I remember one of them being in Top Shop.

There was a lot of competition around for young bands with heartthrob qualities back then and it's just a shame that their record label didn't hook them up with powerful songwriters which could have made them superstars. I shared many happy days touring with Flintlock and meeting many of the fans, one of whom is Shelley".

TONY PRINCE

Chapter One... The Quirkes of Being a Teenager!

In my 30's I saw an article in a magazine where a woman had banned her 14 year old daughter from going to see a band as she said... quote "My daughter becomes too giggly around these other friends who support the band, and all they do is scream at the boys whenever they come on the TV"..... I instantly replied to the magazine saying,
"I can think of much worse things her daughter could be doing at 14!!! Almost three decades ago, I myself was a giggly teenager, screaming at a band, and I don't regret one second of it. I came away from that time with adventures galore, some of the best memories and lovely friends".
Here I am even more years on from that magazine article, and as I recall my young teenage years in the 1970's, I still have the circle of girls I 'screamed along with' in my life. We may all be parted by distance, but due to text, emails and social networks, we are never far away from each other.
So...here's 'our' story, from my point of view, courtesy of several of my diaries, notepads and scrapbooks.
You may want to know who we were screaming at? Well that was an Essex based band called 'Flintlock'. Who? Flintlock.... Ok, I admit, not as big as the 'Rollers' who were also around at this time, but never the less, we fans were still as devoted. You know, even typing that name makes me smile, seriously, these were some of the happiest days of my life.
I, along with the other 'girls' first became aware of Flintlock in the mid 70's, when a program called 'You Must Be Joking' hit our TV screens. It was an energetic, comedic and entertaining program for teens, by teens! If I remember correctly there was only one adult in it, the now infamous 'look at what you could've won' comedian Jim Bowen of 'Bullseye' fame. I for one, can clearly recall the first time I saw the band, I was mesmerized, and it's

hard to be mesmerized over beans on toast let me tell you (that's what my Mum had served up for the 'after school' meal). Why would I remember this? Well this was the day when my life changed. Mike (the very cute drummer) was in a close up on the TV dressed very angelic! And then the music kicked in. I instantly loved it, I loved them, I loved the program. I wasn't so keen on the beans on toast! From then on, my main aim in life was to hurry home from school once a week, plant myself firmly in front of the TV, and worship this band. Yes, Mike Holoway (drums and vocals) Derek Pascoe (lead vocals and saxophone) John Summerton (guitar and vocals) Bill Rice (keys and backing vocals) and Jamie Stone (bass and backing vocals) had, without their knowing, become as important to me as breathing. While I still did all my school work, concentrated the best I could in each class, and tried to make the parents proud etc, I can't deny 'Flintlock' had become an everyday thought pattern. What had occupied my life before these five down to earth boys from Dagenham had emerged? Absolutely no idea. Looking back, it got silly. But hey, I was a little teenager you're allowed to be silly at that age surely. Mum and I would go into the town (my 'town' being Nottingham) and go to a café as a treat, and the phrase from a waitress when ordering "Er, would you like chips or rice with that" would send me into a happiness melt down "owww rice, RICE! That's Bill's name"…………yes, it got that bad. My life revolved around school and Flintlock, Flintlock and school. Pocket money fueled my addiction, and as 'You Must Be Joking' became more popular, so did the boy's and they soon started to spring up regularly in teen magazines.

Yes, my pocket money was devoted to my interest, and if there was a magazine with the boys in it, then I HAD to have it, no matter how small the picture was, or how little the article, I felt unfaithful if I didn't get it! 'Jackie' magazine was a house delivered treat on a regular basis, a birthday gift from my Mum, and the boys became fixtures as in posters, and interviews most editions. There was also the 'three purchase rule' too. If there was a magazine, let's say 'Mates' for example, with an exceptional poster in the centre, then three copies it had to be. One would go on the bedroom wall. One to cover a school book and one to just..... 'have'. I recall my Dad saying to me one week, "Why don't you buy something else with ya money, in six months' time you'll have forgotten about these lads and wondered where ya money went". How dare he. As it happened, they didn't disappear in those 6 months, nor did my interest, and even though, yes, my pocket money did disappear on anything, and EVERYTHING to do with Flintlock, the upside was, my Mum didn't have to decorate my bedroom for almost four years due to just about every inch of it being wallpapered with posters of the boys.

I wasn't the first girl to act like this over a band, or singer. Many before me had screamed and swooned over the likes of Elvis and The Beatles, and even though 3 years before at the very grown up age of 10, I was going weak at the knee's, at the sight of David Cassidy on TV in The Partridge Family (aka the prettiest man ever!)........With 'Flintlock' however, something different was happening, for a start they were my age! And looked like handsome versions of the boys I was at school with, and talented, and more importantly.......lived here, in England!

As YMBJ came to an end, my interest didn't, it grew and grew and grew. It even got to the point where I'd programmed the lady in the newsagents so well, I would go in before school with my friend Jane, and I'd be informed as to recent magazine appearances. One particular visit for example went... "Hello duck, thought you might like to know, that there group you like Flintlarks! Are in FAB208"..........Flintlarks! Flintlarks!!! I allowed her that, she was very old, almost 40! And the fact was, Flintlarks! 'were' in FAB208, so I left the shop a very happy girl. It was around this time we had our first 'party-line' house phone.

So basically my Saturday's would revolve around going to town with friends, buying magazines with Flintlock in, talking to friends about Flintlock, and then going home, to phone friends, to talk about...yes!!!! 1976 Flintlock truly infested my year, from start to finish.

During this time via a magazine, which I believe was 'Look -In' (of which a relatively short time after this they also had their own comic strip in) I joined the 'Flintlock Fan Club', I never looked back. It opened up a whole new world to me. I received a lovely welcome letter, picture of the boys and my fan club number was 1888. Firstly, Sue asked (Sue was the fan club secretary...in later times Maureen took over holding the reigns.) 'Would any fans like to become pen pals with each other from different parts of the country, interact, talk about the boys, share experiences'.........'Er YES, I did, I did! So with that, I wrote in. I think it was only a couple of weeks later I'd had a reply, with a name and address. My pen pal was to be Lynne Tuvey, who lived in Surrey, and in turn Lynne had received 'my' details. Days, yes days after getting the name of my 'flinty' pen pal..........her first letter arrived.

It was a Friday, and I was just about to leave the house for school. I opened up the letter and out fell a photograph of herself, with Mike!..............WHAT. SHE'D MET THEM! I still have that letter and photo, and even now on the very rare occasions that I read it, it still fills me with the excitement it did back then, obviously in a different way, but the emotions are easily recalled. I can still hear the crackle of our coal fire and see the orange flowers on the wallpaper of our sitting room as if it were yesterday. At that time that innocent little letter was one of the most special things to happen to me. I was so happy, so so happy. Our friendship blossomed, the letters went back and forth on a weekly basis, as did the photos, the amazing, fabulous photos. Lynne lived 'darrrn sarrff', so Flintlock we're a lot more accessible to her than me living up in the East Midlands. During

this time of getting to know each other, we also found out that there was to be a new program featuring the boys called 'Pauline's Quirkes', to be aired on ITV.....remember, back in the 70's we only had the three channels, so this was a big deal.
15th November 1976. First episode of Pauline's Quirkes.
The day arrived, although I think they had just come out, we didn't have a video recorder, so it was all the more important to get home from school and get the best seat in the house in front of the TV to take in every second of this new show. Pauline had come hot foot from the YMBJ stable and was this bright and confident 16 year old. Well, we all know how that story went from strength to strength. Her resident band Flintlock (her Quirkes!) featured in the program every week as the house band, and they would also take part in the sketches, some of which were even written by Bill Rice. After the first episode, which didn't disappoint by the way, it would be a regular thing to race home and sit directly in front of the TV, holding a small microphone wired up to my 'Dansette' cassette player! How else was I going to enjoy the music once the program had finished?!!!!
I think it was also that day I discovered quite by chance I could multi-task! As the program began my Mum was chirping in the background "So which one is Bill then?" "And who's that one on the guitar"?, yes, not only could I still watch, listen and enjoy, I found I could also with ease, answer every question aimed at me.
Pauline's Quirkes had a live studio audience, and crikey were they live!!! My 'new' friend Lynne and her group of friends were often present in the audience, usually at the front! Waving hands, scarves anything that would draw attention to themselves really, calling for their faves in the band……..it was all very intense!
I only managed to go to one filming of P.Q's during its second series. Due to transport stopping and starting on a very irregular basis, I was late and so when I reached the studio everyone was in….including my friend I'd arranged to meet there, and the doors

were closed. I think my genuine tears and hang dog look had an effect on the doorman at the studio who said "owww come on love, follow me". And even though I had to sit on the back row………I was in, yeh.

Here's what some of the girls (aka 'Flinties') have to say about that time……

"The first time I saw Flintlock on YMBJ, I loved their music. The sketches were fun, but the music shone through. I used to watch the show with my fellow Flintlock friend, Elizabeth (Lovell) after doing homework and waiting for her parents to come home. I just liked them, and their music despite the bizarre clothes at times!! I wasn't complaining though. Regarding Pauline's Quirkes, this was an adventure, as I managed to get 4 tickets for a show. It ended up being the 'Strip The Clothes Off' show! The tickets were for me, Elizabeth, plus our foreign exchange students. We had traveled from Sheffield, driven by Elizabeth's Dad. We did the whistle stop sights of London before heading to Teddington Studios (Thames TV). Our exchange students then decided they didn't want to go and went all 'mardy' on us! Thank goodness for Mr. Lovell.

I don't remember meeting many fans that day, as timings were tight. But I enjoyed the show, lots of excitement and scarf waving. Unfortunately I was further back in the audience, due to all the kerfuffle getting there"!

…as told by Lynne Brown

"YMBJ was my 'first' at seeing them perform, but I'd met them properly outside no.55 (Derek's house) with a girl named Pauline Griffiths who had the most amazing hair and was a huge Mike fan. We only knew where Derek and Mike lived, but thanks to a group of girls we met who were already outside Derek's place we soon found out where the others were".
…as told by Fran Norton

"The first time I saw Flintlock was when me and my friend went to London to see YMBJ being recorded. We were so pleased we'd managed to get tickets. How we got there and back I have no idea!!? All I do remember was Mike singing 'Learn to Cry', bliss".
…as told by Grace Hargreaves

"I first saw them was on YMBJ. I fell madly in love with Mike, so my friend and I decided to find him. Off to the phone box we went and looked up Mike's name, we then phoned him up and had a chat and asked if we could come and see him on Saturday!!! He said 'Yes', so we did, knocked on the door, and there he was. He was cleaning out his fish tank if I remember rightly, then that was it for the next few years, it was all about the band".
…as told by Linda White

"Saw them on first 'You Must Be Joking' and loved them instantly. I decided there and then that I would obviously marry Mike! I wrote to 'Thames Television' to ask for tickets for the show. My memories from that day, sitting on the wall outside Teddington, making new friends with other fans and swapping names and addresses. Going inside the studio and feeling so

excited I could hardly breathe. Then seeing the boys in the flesh for the first time was overwhelming. To top it all we met Pauline at Waterloo station on our way home".
…as told by Ann French

"My 'first' was YMBJ, actually at the studios. They were far more easily accessible than 'Slick', 'Sweet', or 'The Bay City Rollers'. Thames TV became our new home! And Bill was my crush. I so wanted to marry him back in the day, but he clearly missed the boat there".
…as told by Lorraine Vickers-Bennett

"The first time I took notice of Flintlock was on YMBJ… *thud*… it was love at first sight. I was at my friend Julie's house and when the guys started to sing, wow did I take notice of them. I remember saying how I fancied John and look how cute his bottom was! and Julie went for Bill. The following week we asked another friend Sherrie if we could watch the program at her house (as she had colour TV)… and that's when I fell in love with Derek. Never at that moment would I have thought what these guys would mean to me"!
…as told by Pauline Vincent

FLINTLOCK are the greatest, Flintlock really rule,
But Summerton's the loveliest, the best one of them all.
Derek is the saxman, his singing's really great,
But John Boy is the only one, I really love and hate.
Billy Whizz the keyboard king, makes me really laugh.
When someone knocks on Michael's door, he's always in the bath.
Jamie plays the bass guitar, and Mike beats on the drum.
Together these boys make FLINTLOCK, in my heart they're number one.

……………………………………… By Helen Morris 1977

So, I wasn't the only one who loved…….and I mean truly loved this band. During the weeks of Pauline's Quirkes airing on the TV, I had some mail from Lynne that, well, never in a million years did I ever think would happen. I was a young teenager, things like this didn't happen to kids like me……….or did they? Lynne started off the letter "I know it's not my turn to write Shelley, and I know it's only a few weeks' notice but I was wondering, would you like to come to see the boys in concert at The New Victoria Theatre the first weekend in December, I've spoken to my Mum and your welcome to stay at my house". Ohhhhhh…….'the hills are alive with the sound of music, arrrhhhhhh'……….my head was singing, it was spinning, it was everything that could be described as wonderful. I read out the letter to my Mum and Dad who were sitting at the table having breakfast. Without a single thought for the idea (it seemed) my Mum replied, "Oh well, never mind there will be other times"…….and 'CRASH'……..Other times? other times??? Why can't 'this' just be, 'a time'? My singing, spinning, wonderful world had just been crushed. I was dumb founded, I had no words. Answering back was never an option, but this was the most important thing in the world……ever, and even if I had wanted to backchat!! I actually had no words. Everything went into some kind of surreal alternative world, and as I heard the two of them discussing all the reasons why it wouldn't, and couldn't happen, I found myself saying "Ta-ra then"…………..and as if in a very grey foggy haze, I left for school. There was no consoling me, I cried all the way there, cried during breaks, cried during dinner, and cried all the way home! My friends were ever supportive, even if, they didn't really get it. Most had already started on 'real-life' boyfriends, wearing make-up, and generally being the 18 year olds in their heads that they actually were, so my dilemma was trivial by comparison. As a rule I didn't mind school, but this day seemed like a lifetime. The school bell did eventually ring, and it was time to go home. I remember walking through my front door feeling sick, I hadn't had dinner. How could I eat when my heart was broken, yes it was that serious, and I'd cried all day, it felt like a full time job! I hung my coat up and could hear the parents laughing in the sitting room. Laughing at a time like this, my life had practically ended and 'they' were laughing! "Shelley is that you" Mum called. My teenage angst wanting to come back with some sharp and witty answer but I had nothing. "Come in here duckie" she continued, "we want to talk to you". I walked into the sitting room resembling Eeyore. Both Mum and Dad sat there giving me that 'parent' look. "Right then" Dad sighed, "this 'ere group ya mad about, 'IF' we let you go and see them in this concert, there will be a few rules". Eh, had I heard that right? I checked before allowing the music to take over my head, "You mean, you er, you mean"....."arrh" said Dad, "We are thinking of letting you go, but as I said there will be rules make no mistake about that young lady"………..' YES! …..the hills are alive………etc'……….the singing, spinning, wonderful world was back. Standing still wasn't an option at this point. I would've made Gene Kelly looks static. "Thankyouuuuuu" I grinned. "So" Mum began quite seriously, "I've been on the phone this afternoon to Lynne's Mum, Rose, what a lovely lady, anyway she said she and Lynne will meet you at the station on the Friday, so you'll have to have a day off school" (this concert just kept getting better and better) "and then they would take you back to the station to get your train Sunday, I'll go with you Friday to get your train. BUT, you must phone me when you get to the station, do what Lynne's parents say and remember your manners, don't talk to any strange men and……….." she carried on through my Dad barking "Oh that's enough now, she's not stupid our 'Blue' (pet name)….now then, don't let us down eh, we are trusting you to be sensible". Within an hour of that fantastic parent to child conversation I was on the phone to Lynne. I guess it's hard to imagine in this day and age of private phone lines and mobiles, but we were on a party line with three other neighbours. I was half way through a very excitable 'first' conversation with Lynne, when I heard a voice say "Doreen, is that you"? It was the old lady from across the road, Mrs. Fletcher, thinking her departed sister was trying to contact her via the phone, so I called out for Mum, and she kindly nipped over the road to rescue the situation. At the time we girls chuckled about it for all of five seconds before getting back to the nitty gritty of the concert. However thinking back and now being at this age, awww, It makes me feel sad, that poor lady, she was a very sweet neighbour................Yes we chatted our way through half an hour of 'Flint-talk', and all the exciting things that 'might' happen on the 5th December. Never had a single date meant so much to me. When I came off the phone, there was another surprise for me. As this was such an important event Mum and Dad had decided I could have one of my main Christmas gifts a little early. A Kodak camera complete with square flashbulbs to take with me so that I could take photos of this momentous occasion.

At this time Flintlock had an album out called 'Flintlock....On The Way', which of course I had, so after the phone-chat-camera-giving fest, I went to my room and played it until it resembled onion rings. The following day, Mum and I went into town and booked my train ticket. It was happening. I was actually going to see Flintlock in concert.

Chapter Two... Stupenderific!

Friday 4th December, and my adventure began. Tickets booked, arrangements made, concert ticket reserved, bags packed and excitement stored in stomach! Yes, everything was as it should be. Mum and I traveled by taxi (posh eh) to Nottingham train station. I'd only ever been on a train once before this, two years previous actually when my elder brother Steve decided I should go on one as 'they were great'! So he treated me to a trip. Nottingham to Long Eaton! And back again. I think it's approximately 14 miles round trip! But at the time, it was like going to America....as in, a long way and very exciting! Talking of the elder bro, I'm sure he had a hand in persuading Mum to allow me to go to London in the first place, she as much admitted it to me as I approached my 20's, and there was I thinking I'd only been brought into the world to argue and bicker with him! Anyhow, I digress. It wasn't long before we'd reached the station and got onto the platform that my train pulled in for St. Pancras Station, London. The 9.50am train, how could I forget that? As the doors opened and we stepped forward my Mum said with a little tremor in her voice "sit next to a lady if you can". "Alright" I replied and got on the train. My knees were shaking and I was full of excitement and nerves. I'd never traveled so far on my own before, so this was a weekend full of firsts. As instructed I 'found a lady' and sat facing her and her young toddler within seconds of getting on the train. I looked out of the window, Mum was standing near the window with a brave smile, "have you got a clean hankie" she mouthed and gestured towards my bag "yes" I said a little embarrassed. I didn't want this mother opposite me to think I'd never been on a train on my own before, I was practically an adult wasn't I? After all I was on my way to see a band in concert. "Is this your first time on a train on your own"? The lady asked. "Yes" I said instantly. Umm so much for the cool exterior. She struck up a conversation. "Where are you off to"? "London" I said, "Oh I get off the stop before, but we can keep each other company until then", she said. Even though my stomach was doing loop-de-loops, I instantly felt more at ease, and I think with hindsight the lady could sense my Mum's worry and had taken some sort of lead towards comforting her thoughts. The guard began to announce our train's destination and with that it began to pull out. Mum stood on the platform waving. I waved excitedly and mouthed, "I'll be alright, don't worry". I later (much later, as in years later) found out she cried all the way home on the bus, she said "you looked so little on that huge train, and I couldn't believe I'd allowed it, it was just you growing up I 'spose".

Two hours, ten minutes! That was the journey time on the train. For the best part the friendly lady and I chatted. She said "That's very grown up, going to see a group. I doubt my parents would've ever allowed that when was your age. I liked The Hollies you see. So what's so special about Flintlock then" she asked. First of all, was she a mind reader? She pointed to me "your badge". Oh silly me, forgot I'd got my official 'Flintlock' badge on. Lynne and I had agreed to wear our badges so we would recognize each other at the station. I then went on a complete 'sell' of why the band we're so special. Before I knew it the lady announced "Right then, this is my stop, enjoy yourself, have a wonderful time and take-care Shelley, it was nice to meet you". And back came the loop-de-loops of the stomach, now I really was on my own.

Ten minutes after her departure I too was getting off the train. I'd only ever been to London once before on a school trip. Everything was taller, wider, louder than Nottingham, including the people! It surprised me how I managed to walk down the platform with such shaky knees! Honestly, why people didn't point me out shouting, 'look at her, she looks like Bambi'. But they

didn't. It was more in my mind than my knees! Then I spotted my friend Lynne. There she was looking around, almost as lost as me, but obviously not as she was with her Mum. I waved, they waved back, knees stopped shaking. We rushed towards each other and said "awwww, eeee, awww, eeee" hugged and giggled a lot. Lynne's Mum suggested we get a coffee before heading back to Wimbledon. On arriving at Lynne's home her parents Rose and Ken ('Mum and Dad Tuvey') and younger sister Debbie, made me feel very welcome, and before dinner, Lynne and I went up to her room to chat about arrangements for the following day, look at her photos of the boys etc. Her room, just like mine at home, was a shrine to the boys. We chatted, compared notes, laughed and laughed and laughed. Just before dinner, Lynne's Mum tapped on the bedroom door and said "Shelley, have you forgotten something"? I didn't think so, I had my scarf, camera, spending money, er……..oh no! I'd forgotten to phone my Mum! As it happened that was why Rose was reminding me as my Mum was on the phone and had been reassured by 'Mum Tuvey' that "all was well, Shelley had arrived safe and sound and the girls were getting along great". I rushed downstairs to speak to Mum. Oddly enough I didn't get the roasting I was expecting. Instead, "hello duckie, are you having a lovely time"? "Yes thank you" I replied "I'm sorry I made you worry, it's just really exciting" I said. "Yes, ya Dad said it would be that, alright then, be careful won't you, and 'don't' forget to phone me Sunday, enjoy yourself duckie". That night I don't actually remember sleeping, Lynne and I were far too giddy and chatted/slept/chatted/slept the night away, Flintlock style!
Morning arrived and as we ventured downstairs for breakfast Lynne's parents presented her with an early Christmas gift, a Kodak camera, complete with square flashbulbs!!! How cool were our parents back then. Very! Before we left we had our first official photograph together outside her house. On leaving to

head for London, we were instructed with all the same rules I'd been given previously. We met up with other members of the 'Wimbledon Gang', Gill, Lorraine, Terry, Lisa and Julie.

The train journey into London was an experience in itself. To get to London we traveled by train in a single carriage type, and all I can remember about that was Lorraine climbing into the luggage rack overhead and the rest of us laughing uncontrollably!!! Everything seemed so fast and thrilling.

Here's a little piece directly out of my diary from back then, and just so you're aware, Lorraine was a 'Bill fan'.

"I really like Lorraine, I hope one day she marries Bill"

Everything seemed pretty straight forward at that age……..
We decided, on arriving in London that as this was a Christmas concert we would buy some purple tinsel (purple was the colour of the bands car, 'Flinty') to wrap around our heads, wrists, waists. This is partly what I'd written word for word in my diary for this date.

"Well, I can tell you I was pretty nervous as it was the first time I'd seen Flintlock. We waited outside the New Victoria Theatre and saw the support group 'Rocky' arrive. Then came Mr. Holoway, Mr. Summerton, Mr. Stone, Mrs. Holoway and Mike's sisters. The big moment came at five minutes to 1pm. 'Flinty' (the car!) pulled up and Mike and Bill jumped out and ran up the steps to the doors, but they were locked, I took a photo. They came down the steps and Mike rushed by us towards the stage door. Lynne called "Mike, this is the friend I told you about, my pen pal from Nottingham, Shelley, well here she is" and pulled me forwards. He said "hello, thanks for traveling down" then asked me if I was alright about five times, cor, he's really nice. I turned around and grabbed hold of what I thought was Lynne, it wasn't it was Derek, he said "ello, she's gotta hold of me" and gave me this lovely smile, he is so nice and I think I have a crush. Lynne told Derek my name and he said "hello Shelley from Nottingham". This is the bestest day.

Alright, I grant you, it's not exactly Anne Frank! But I just said it as it was, and for me it was 'The Bestest Day'.
The rest of the afternoon, we walked up and down past the theatre and back again, around, and around, and around. Now this sounds boring, and no doubt it would be now, but then it was just the build up to 'who knows'. Meeting up with other flinty-fans, some of which the girls knew, and others which none of us knew, but as the day went on we kinda did! The excitement just kept building. I have to say these were some of the friendliest girls I'd ever met in my life. We all had the same aim, to see the boys, shout, scream, cheer, and hopefully come away from our experience with a head full of achieved dreams.
We ventured into a 'Wimpy', and we all crammed ourselves around two tables. I remember ordering chips, but got through five and couldn't face anymore. I was far too excited to eat. So it was just a coke for me, and Julie, assisted by Lorraine, finished off the chips. During this 'walk-a-bout' time, we had purchased flowers for the boys, Lynne, Lisa and I getting Carnations for Mike, and the girls also getting flowers for their 'men'. Five o'clock arrived and more fans were starting to arrive outside the theatre. I found it fascinating listening to 'my' girls saying things like "Oh look there's Grace from Birmingham and her mate", and "Hiya" waving across to flint-made-friends from areas of Essex. It was all suddenly feeling very real. We hung around the stage door, just in case! One of Mike's sisters, Debbie had come out, so we wrapped notes around our flower-gifts and she kindly took them back in for us to pass onto the boys.
For two hours before the doors opened, we 'camped' in front of the theatre doors singing a mish mash medley of Flintlock songs. The girl at the side of me offered me an Opal Fruit, and then we

chatted about the boys as if we'd known each other for years! The number of fans continued to increase, and it was also apparent that there were quite a lot of police now patrolling around to keep us in order. Although, I don't recall any trouble, all I do remember regarding the police, were them asking us about Flintlock then cheekily taking the mickey out of them! The atmosphere was fantastic, there were now hundreds of girls outside the theatre and dare I say, standing at the very front, I felt a bit smug! But to hear a few hundred girls all singing 'Flintlock's On The Way', was something I will never forget. A great experience and this was still outside! I kept thinking "I'm going to burst with excitement, and we haven't even got in the place yet". Some of the fans got a little over excited shall we say and decided to climb up a drainpipe.

"Me and my friend climbed up the drainpipe and managed to get onto the roof! Got into trouble with the manager of the venue and he banded us from going in. I remember sitting on the steps and crying so much, then Mike's Dad came by and asked us what was wrong, and he got us back in. Crazy or what".
…as told by Grace Hargreaves

Suddenly some ushers from inside the theatre walked towards the doors, the doors were open and yes, we were in. It was like the start of a race, even though we all had seat allocations, if you got in sooner you were that bit closer to the concert happening right!
I'd been to theatres before to see shows but never a concert, and this had a totally different feel to the place. The stage was set for a start with instruments, and that alone for me was exciting. I thought my heart was going to pound right out of my chest, the lights, the sounds, and excitement in the air was

electric. Lynne and the Wimbledon Gang had front row seats, and I was right behind them on the second row! They got their tickets before my fate had been decided by the parents you see. Anyhow in a place the size of The New Vic, I think second row was pretty good, and possibly lucky to get it as it was a single ticket. The ticket prices were £1, £1.75 and £2.50. The stage was set with silver Christmas trees, and the front of the stage was decorated with…….bouncers! Yes, there were so many girls it was inevitable that the concert required security. Lynne turned around, "Shelley, climb over the seat, you can sit between me and Lisa, and besides, when the show starts we will all be up at the front". Should I? Could I? Would I? Yes, I did…….as I climbed over the front row of seats a rather buff looking gent strolled over to me and the girls. "Now come on girls, what's going on here" he asked. "Oh please let my friend sit with us at the front" pleaded Lynne, "No love, get back to your seat" he demanded, "but, but, but she's come all the way from Australia to visit and she's never seen the boys before" she said. And with that I put on the most unconvincing Australian accent, "souuu true mayte" I said, trying to sound and even look Australian!!! He stood and starred at me, which seemed like hours, it was probably 7 seconds. "Go on then", he sighed "but no trouble and no getting up onto the stage". "Ha" I thought at the time, "peerreeettty good accent there Shelley, fooled him". Looking back, what was I thinking!!! Of course I hadn't fooled him, he was just looking at me thinking 'really' and probably just had pity on me. Either way I got the result I wanted and there I was with my girls on the front row, yippee. The atmosphere was buzzing, a very new experience for me, so I drank in every second of it. Suddenly, the lights went down………and the screams went up!!!! The sound of the screams seemed to hit the back wall and then come back over our heads like a wave of sound, so hard to explain if you have never experienced it. Ridiculously intense and something I

could never have previously comprehended. I'd never heard a sound like it in such a high pitch. I didn't join in, why were they screaming like that? Why would I want to do that, even though the lack of lights and the screaming was rather exciting. At this point, we had maneuvered ourselves right in front of the stage where we were sandwiched in. It's easy to see how fans faint at concert's there really was no breathing space, at all!!!!
Newton Wills, Flintlocks tour/publicity manager walked out onto the stage to introduce the show and then the support band 'Rocky'. We all danced and shouted off a little of our energy. After they had done they're bit there was a ten minute interval and then the lights went down again, this time the screams were absolutely piercing, DJ Tony Prince, (and president of the fan club) walked out onto the stage and introduced Flintlock, by doing a little chant with the audience, as in "Who do you want"? ……..and we would shout back "Flintlock". I remember the melody of 'Silbury Hill' (an album track) playing as the excitement built. Then the moment came, the lights illuminated, and right in front of my eyes the boys were on the stage. WOW!!!! I, along with every other red blooded girl in that audience screamed like my life depended on it, what a release! I'd never done that before!!! The music was loud, as were the audience, and the boys fought to be louder than us. It was by far, the most exhilarating experience I'd ever had. Yeh, yeh, I was only a kid, so not a lot to compare it to. That aside, I screamed, I laughed, I swayed, I hugged fellow fans, I was in a fabulous little bubble, I sang along with each and every song and ached with that "Owww I'd love to be able to do that on stage one day" feeling. I was in a dream, here I was listening to all the songs I'd become so familiar with in my little bedroom at home, and now, right now, here 'they' were, actually performing all those songs, right in front of me, ME! I was there, 'with' the people who occupied my head on a

daily basis! In the same building, a matter of feet away!!! Arrrrrhhhhhhhkkkk….. (That was me screaming!)

Close to the end of the show, Flintlock left the stage and the fans went c-r-a-z-y. Tony and Newton came back onto the stage and were joined by Sally James (of 'Tiswas' TV show) the boys joined them after a bit of banter, and the Christmas spirit was alive and well at The New Vic, as balloons and artificial snow fell onto the audience and Flintlock sang 'Carry Me'…….arms were waved, as was our recently purchased tinsel and many cried, we knew we'd have to part company soon. The boys were in a dreamy mist of 'fog' …'arrrh, this must be what heaven feels like', were my thoughts. I was within feet of Derek singing this, and I'm sure he sang it just to me and me alone…..No? Well it felt like that, and surely at the time that was all that mattered. The concert did indeed end, the boys fled from the stage and had I have been selling tissues then I would be a millionaire. Ninety percent of the audience we're in floods of tears, and the bright auditorium lights were saying 'time to get out'. Bouncers were collectively ushering us out like a heard of sheep with quips of "come on girls, I wanna get home for me supper". I have no doubt this was true, but didn't they understand the emotions we were going through at that very moment? Obviously not!

I floated out of the theatre. I'd just had the best day/night of my life. Vinyl was all well and good, but Flintlock we're even better 'live'.

We decided to wait outside the stage door, but so did every other fan, so we casually slithered around to the main doors trying not to draw attention to ourselves. There our group of girls were scattered with around 10 others. We decided whilst waiting and waiting some more, to have some group-fan photos taken. Just after this and what seemed like endless waiting, the boys rushed out and dived into the car. We too rushed after said car and chased it along the road. Strange what you remember, but I do! The car went past, ultimately so did we, The Victoria Theatre. It was advertising the Pantomime there, Aladdin! Starring Kenneth Connor and 'Diddy' David Hamilton! That's all I have to say about that! But I do remember it!! All too soon, the car sped off without us…………………….and that was that. We were teary, and giggly, and back in the real world, and so we made our way back to Wimbledon. The train journey on the return wasn't as noisy at it had been going to the concert. We were screamed out…but content. Back at Lynne's home with the concert still alive and ringing in our ears, we sat telling her mum all about our fabulous day's adventure. She sat smiling and nodding along as we chatted ten to the dozen covering every last detail. She then disappeared into the kitchen and came back with chicken sandwiches and tea. I don't drink tea as a rule, but it was the best drink I'd ever tasted.

I've always said how that was one of the best days of my life, and all these years on, nothing has changed, it still is up there in the top ten of amazing days.

Here are a few more memories from the girls of that fabulous concert.

"…the New Vic was one of the best nights I'd ever had, that was the night I climbed up the drainpipe at the side of the theatre! That was also the concert I met Grace (Birmingham), she was sitting in front of me. I also remember screaming and crying so much, I was carried out. I begged them to let me back in again. Fortunately there was a distraction and I ran like hell back in before they could stop me".

…as told by Pauline Vincent

"Screamed so much I was carried out for some air by the stewards. Good gig though".
...as told by Lorraine Vickers-Bennett

"I was there with my friend June, first gig we'd been to. 'So' excited, got there about 10am, met Michelle, Sue, Lorraine and Amanda outside. The boys turned up early afternoon, I grabbed a couple of photos (black and white!). June and I even developed the photos at school in art class. The main thing I remember about the actual concert was the anticipation before they came on stage, screaming like I'd never screamed before! Singing along to everything and making new friends. It was a great day. From then on there was no stopping us".
...as told by Ann French

"I so remember this. We were really excited about seeing the boys arrive. I'd been well coached by Ann on the songs and had been watching them on TV too".
...as told by June Sims

"I went to the New Vic with my friend Julie. I think this is the one where they were singing 'Learn To Cry', and the fog machine went hay wire, and it totally covered the stage, so we could hardly see them, I remember hearing the boys laughing though. It was really funny and a great concert".
...as told by Linda White

The following day was home day for me. First things first, the dutiful phone call to Mum!!! Then Lynne and her Mum came to the station with me, and we hugged and said our goodbyes and cried a little, and Lynne's Mum said "Please come and see us again won't you Shelley". I squeaked "yes, I'd like that, thank you" and then cried a bit more. All the way home I kept re-living my 'Fan'tastic weekend, reliving the memories, the fun and looking at my keepsake tickets. Had all that really just happened? Yep, it had, so I relived it some more. Getting to Nottingham station I spied my brother Steve waiting for me. I couldn't really have a conversation with him as Id screamed my voice away! Eventually as it got darker we arrived home, and Mum greeted me at the front door "Oh hello duckie, I have missed you" she beamed. "Have you had a lovely time then" she asked with a huge smile on her face. "Stupenderific" I croaked, still a bit teary. "Eh" she replied. "Stupenderific" I squeaked in a pitch only dogs could hear. She looked at me, frowned a little and then said "ohhhh, stupendous and terrific together, oh I see, umm Stupenderific it is then". And you know what? It really was.

Chapter Three... Those Non-Event-Events!

Every now and again, life with Flintlock wasn't always straight forward, and so now and again we would experience some 'Non Event-Events'! Let me explain. These were the times when despite planning everything to the finest detail, sometimes the universe had other ideas.
Since the Christmas 'New Vic' concert life in the Flint-lane had gone up a notch, pen-pals were a plenty, correspondence had increased and so had the phone bills. So it was only a matter of time before another encounter with Flintlock was going to happen, or was it? April 10th 1977. This was my second trip down to Lynne's. The boys had been advertised to appear as part of Battersea Park's Parade. There were quite a collection of us at this gathering as Gill's pen-pal Viv from Sheffield in Yorkshire, and Terry's pen-pal Karen from Pontefract also in Yorkshire were joining the gang, so nine of us in all. As previously arranged we met up before hand and after a selection of train hopping connections arrived at Battersea Park. Capital Radio had an open top bus and the idea was, I'm guessing, that the boys go upstairs on the bus and as it drove around the parks circuit they would wave to fans and the parade audience alike! I say I'm guessing as it never actually happened! We arrived quite early, the Capital Radio bus and stand was just 'warming up' so to speak. Playing records and holding competitions. Viv got up onto the stage to dance and Lorraine was in a competition where you couldn't say 'yes' or 'no'. Both of them accumulating radio logo freebies for doing so, I also remember T-Shirts being given out. One of my distinctive memories that day was actually just after this and Lorraine making a bee-line for the bouncy castle with a couple of other fans, and before we could say "don't forget to take your shoes off" there she was, bouncing about like a, well, a very bouncy thing! There was never a dull moment when you were lucky

enough to be in Lorraine's company. Soon after this highly entertaining episode I spotted the arrival of 'Grace from Birmingham' in a tee-shirt that read 'Mike luvs Grace' on it. The fact was you didn't have to see Grace and her friend Marie to realize they'd arrived anywhere, you heard Grace first. It was like a war-cry "MIKE, IT'S GRACE FROM BIIIIRRRMINGHAM". Not so long ago, a few of us were chatting about this on 'Face book' actually with Grace, and friend Ann said (quote) *"I always thought I was quite loud until I met Grace"*. Yes, Grace was never a shy and retiring fan and she would be the first one to admit that.

Not quite sure to this day what exactly happened at the park back then, but there seemed to be some kind of detour caused by some Bay City Roller fans, so a lot of the girls ran towards a random car that they were led to believe Flintlock were in. In fact there were many fans of 'various band worship' at the park that day and they seemed to be going in every conceivable direction like ants! I, along with Viv and Lisa stayed close by the Capital Radio bus, after all this is where the boys were heading for when they did actually arrive. Suddenly Lisa said "ooohhh look they're here" and 'Flinty' came around the corner and I noticed Bill, Jamie and Derek inside. We were the only ones quite close by so we scuttled towards the car and within seconds swarms of fans just seemed to come from nowhere. 'Flinty' was being followed by a second car with the other boys in, and as it was being swallowed up by fans I remember Mike's Dad, 'Big Mick', standing up in the car (as in leaning right out of the window of course!!! He didn't have super powers!!!)... shouting, "you all need to move out of the way, back away from the cars girls, we don't want any injuries, if you don't back away we will have to go home". Well, this fell on deaf ears, if anything the girls went even wilder. The car kept edging back and forth, back and forth, trying to gently push through the sea of screaming girl's. But it wasn't going to happen. Girls were not only covering the cars around the side, but climbing on the bonnet, boot, etc. I along with Viv we're squashed up against 'Flinty', and even if we'd have wanted to move we couldn't. It was probably then I discovered it's hard to look adorable when your body is flattened up against a car window! It got quite manic and after a short while Big Mick decided to quite rightly get the boys safely out of there. I don't think they had expected quite so many girls, there were a couple of hundred at the very least. The unfortunate thing was, while Big Mick and the other driver of 'Flinty' drove off into the distance. Jamie meanwhile had managed to get out of the first car and onto the top deck of the bus! By now the fans were on a rampage, the cars were driving around Battersea Park with this huge pack of wild fans in hot pursuit. I think it was exciting? In fact I'm sure it was. It must have been. It's just that you don't always make your own mind up at that age in those circumstances, and I found myself running aimlessly after a car too! Talk about getting caught up in the moment. Even as I did it, it felt wrong, and pointless, and soon after having these thoughts I saw a girl go 'splat' onto the gravel path. So I gave up the chase, and along with a couple of the Wimbledon gang we rushed towards her and helped her up. Her hands were cut terribly and so we made our way to the First Aid post. Her name was Linda, and she was also from Nottingham. Small world! Due to this very obscure 'meet' we too became friends. After a while 'our gang' found each other again, and poor Jamie, who'd been stranded on the open top bus was eventually rescued when 'Flinty' come back for him, and yes, I do realize that sounded like Trigger the horse rescuing Roy Rogers the cowboy……….moving on!

So what were we to do now, the boys had come and gone in what seemed like the blink of an eye, and now the parade was starting. So we 'fans' just followed the brightly coloured Capital Radio bus

around the park, and getting more looks than the actual bus as we waved our arms and proudly sang Flintlock songs.
Very innocent by today's standards, but we enjoyed ourselves.

"Met Viv and Karen today, nice girls. I get on very well with Viv, and we have already swapped addresses. Ow running around after the boys, it was daft and I felt daft, running round and laughing and thinking this is daft, why am I doing this. But I did. Picked up a fan who'd fallen over called Linda Beardsley, she was like me from Nottingham. Poor Linda, her hands were really badly cut from her fall, but now we are friends. We are meeting up next week, can't wait, more Flint-friends. We got told off for breaking down a fence, but we didn't do it, so Terry told the security man off for shouting at us. He was horrible. Then he told some Roller fans off and they ran away. I think he actually saw the boys that broke the fence down, but decided not to shout at them".

There was one time Linda (yes, that one.) and I tried to organize a protest outside of Radio One, as they never played 'Flintlock' records. We'd had various letters and requests ignored……..So, we decided to travel down to London armed with our petition of fans names. It was all going so well……..until we actually got there! And discovered for whatever reason, quite possibly a communication cock up, there were only 13 of us that had actually turned up. Ooops. The police, who'd been called in, to keep the 'crowd' under control outnumbered us! Ha ha ha. It's a good thing we had a sense of humour as we laughed about it like drains, and even told the boys about it when we met them later in the day. Oh the shame, but once again it wasn't a total loss, we didn't get a positive radio result, boo. (Even though we did still hand in the impressive petition) but it was sunny and we had a great time in London that day….followed by a mini visit to Dagenham where we managed to see Derek and John, and Jamie.

We experienced other non-event-events like this, but I have to say, they were still enjoyable. Many a time we would travel to Thames TV, (Teddington Lock) and sit on the wall outside the main entrance of the studios all day, and I mean, 'all' day, sometimes only to be treated to a fleeting glance of our boys as the car went through the gate. But it seemed worth it……… no….it really did. If the cars did ever stop, and we were spoken to, well that really was a special day. During these times Mike joined the cast of 'The Tomorrow People', and there were more Pauline's Quirkes being filmed. They were also doing guest appearances on shows like 'Supersonic'. And at a later date Flintlock did get they're very own program called 'Fanfare'. So there were many reasons and opportunities to go to Thames and just 'sit'. Look, to an outsider the obvious question they would ask is "So, you just go to Thames Television, and sit on a wall, waiting"? (You gathered this particular outsider was my Dad yeh!?) And the honest answer is "yes we did". But it was so much more than that. Flintlock, were of course the main source of our interest and addiction, but another massive social aspect of it was 'the fans'. I made friends with people that I'd never have met otherwise from all different areas of the country. Remember back then, no social media. So to meet up with these girls, and the odd boy, (by odd boy, I mean a lone character, not an 'odd' boy!) we would catch up and chat and exchange phone numbers/addresses. The friendship circle became as important as the boys themselves. I would think to anyone who has never experienced that sort of band worship/fan camaraderie would struggle to understand its value and importance, but for those that have, well, no more words are required.

Could I just add while I've spoken about my Dad, he really quite liked the band 'specially after he'd witnessed the first year of my constant dedication. Quite proudly he told the chaps he worked with "Oww our Shelley, she loves that group Flintlock, she's one of the groupies"…………er…….No, no, no, no, no……….no……..and again, no!!!! He almost had a fit when my Mum pointed out exactly what a groupie was…………………*cough*

There was even 'one' time when our reliable Dagenham encounters didn't happen……Yes we went there but on arriving found out 'not one' of the boys was at home. Gulp! From Nottingham it was a fair trek. Even though there was obvious disappointment at not seeing the boys the positive side was meeting up with our flinty friends, and that was also the day I made two new friends called Imelda and Alison from Liverpool. Alison asked me if I had a nail file as we stood outside Derek's pondering what to do next, and the friendship began! We swapped addresses and would often meet up at concerts……personal appearances…….and yes, Dagenham. Bills Mum was also lovely, inviting a couple of us to have a cup of tea. She was worried we'd traveled all the way down from Nottingham and not managed to see the boys, how kind of her. I remember I had a coffee and a doggie cuddle with 'Binky' so the day was not a complete loss.

Myself and Viv went to Pebble Beach recording studios once, I hadn't felt too well, and I should've listened to my Mum as she said I didn't look right, but I insisted I was 'fine'…umm, Mum's are usually right eh. The stupid thing about this was we just went there, without a clue where it actually was!! It was by sheer luck we spotted two girls with 'badges' on in the street and asked them if they knew how to get there. Turns out they were on their way, so we just tagged along. Utter madness. I'd never go somewhere blindly now! I'm sure as you get older you 'over think' stuff, hence why everything seems so easy when your young, you just do it! So…..got to the recording studio after a very dubious journey and within half an hour I felt dreadful. Newton came outside to chat to us (there were several girls there) and he said

"Oh good grief dear you look terrible"….Thanks!!!! He went inside and kindly got me a glass of water, and before long I had to admit I felt so rough, so it was back home. We'd only spent about an hour outside the studio. I felt horrid, and to top it all we'd not even seen the boys. And while I felt so ill, I also felt so sorry for Viv having to go back with me but thankfully she was a real pal and understanding about it all. After a trip to see the doctor the following day it turned out I had acute tonsillitis! Umm didn't feel so cute.

…here are some more memories of the non-event-events!

"I loved Pebble Beach, and it was a prime example of our investigation and tracking skills in finding the boys. Also remember Bill and John throwing pebbles into a bucket to make the sound of rain water…I think it was pebbles".
…as told by June Sims

"I thought it was raisins they threw in the bucket to make the noise? I do remember Mike in his blue dressing gown, and refusing to take it off all day. I loved Pebble Beach".

"Your right Ann, it was raisins, I knew pebbles wasn't right when I wrote it ha ha".
…as told by Ann French and June Sims

"Only went to Pebble Beach once with Lynda Mathews and met up with Ann and June - it was the day Mike wouldn't take off his blue dressing gown. Can't remember the names of most of the studios but remember RG Jones in Wimbledon was a regular haunt, Tooting Bec, one in North London where

Buster and Child also recorded. …….Studios in East London had some really good memories but I think it was the wrong time of the month! 'cos I always seemed to fall out with John there".
…as told by Helen Morris

"I went to a car show, I think it was at Chelmsford or around there somewhere. Mike had just failed his driving test and was judging some classic cars. I was there with Jackie Mayall, and some other fans. We had been to Mike's house just before the show and was chased down the long drive by the dogs…….well….the dogs barked and we ran. Can't remember why, but Jackie was a bit miffed with Mike, think he may have said something to upset her. So she said really loudly 'Dunno why you've got him to judge the cars he failed his driving test'……and I fell about laughing".
…as told by Fran Norton

"Went to a gig with June in Mansfield. When we got there it was heavily snowing. We arrived at the venue to be told by some local fans that the boys had just left to go back to Dagenham so they didn't get stuck in by the snow and the concert was cancelled. So what did we do? Go home to make sure we didn't get stranded anywhere? Nooooo of course we didn't. We went to Dagenham in the snow! Our logic to this was, at least we knew for certain the boys were going to be in. It was freezing and I remember my feet feeling so cold, but we needed our fix of the boys, crazy!
…as told by Ann French

"Yeh, the Mansfield gig, Ann, June, Lauren, Fran and me. Ended up buying french sticks from Tesco as they

were selling them off cheap. Got some photos of us rolling about in the snow somewhere, but can't seem to find them"
...as told by Helen Morris

"Oh Battersea Park, went to that, bit of a confusing day, boys didn't hang about and we stayed in a really old dirty B&B, it was really scarey".
...as told by Grace Hargreaves

"Oh Battersea, such a great day out with the girls. Capital Radio and 'Me' up on the stage with a microphone stuck in front of me face ha ha. Flintlock were OK too, the little bit we saw of them.
Another time the Wimbledon Gang got invited out for dinner with Sue and Newton at an Italian restaurant in Orpington. Me, Terry, Gill, Lisa, Lynne and Julie were excited and was hoping the lads would tip up and surprise us. But they didn't! We found out years later they knew nothing about it, but would have come had they known! Bummer!
We all wore our best grand dad shirts too! I had a spag bol and very nice it was too, all curtesy of the fan club.
...as told by Lorraine Vickers-Bennett

"Carole, Bev and I went on a visit to Pinnacle Records where we met Maureen Waller and her husband Les who ran Flintlock's fanclub at that time. They said how Newton wasn't around as he was in a pantomime in Birmingham playing one of the ugly sisters in Cinderella, so we just spent the morning with Maureen and Les which was nice, then in the afternoon we went to Dagenham".
...as told by Alison Grey

"If I remember rightly, the boys were supposed to be appearing in a Dartford Record Store 'Challenger and Hicks'. Lucky for us we arrived really early only to be told that it had been cancelled but they were still doing Maidstone. So we jumped on a train and arrived just in time to see the guys leave, ha ha. Another time I skipped ballet to go to Dagenham. It was a lovely sunny day and we were sitting on the grass outside Derek's house. We could hear he was in his room playing his saxophone. I had my ballet things with me, and someone asked me if I'd go on my pointe shoes. So there I was prancing and dancing around and Derek walks out, and asks me to carry on. I was so shy. Anyhow he drew a picture of me dancing. The problem was when I got home I had grass stains on my pink satin shoes. My Mum went mad as they were very expensive. I can't remember what I told her as there was no grass near the dance studio, luckily I never got caught out. But my punishment was harsh. But hey, to this day I don't regret a thing, and I'd do it all over again if I had the chance."

…as told by Pauline Vincent

I too never made it to the Mansfield concert………..got so far with my Dad as taxi driver and then due to the bad weather the car just gave up on the outskirts of the town. Our car at that time being 'Sid' the Reliant (we all name our cars yeh?). However, not so reliant that day. So we couldn't get to the theatre and even though we only lived in Nottingham, couldn't get home. So I sat in the car shivering and miserable while Dad walked to a phone box to get his friend to pick us and the car up. I don't remember ever being so pleased to see a dusky blue Bedford van creeping through the snow. As it ploughed its way towards us just past the Papplewick turn off I nervously asked my Dad 'how much was this going to cost'? "Nowt ma duck" came back the reply, "he owes me", and as if previously planned, my Dad during the Summer months had made pal John a garden seat, gratis, and so he did indeed 'owe us one'. He then kindly took my Dad and 'Sid' to the garage a few days later, but again, it was covered by a crazy paving path which had been laid by Dad a few months prior, who needs money! On the way back home from my non-existent concert I was so fed up, until we pulled into a pub car park that is!!! I remember my Dad saying "just need to nip in here". Need? I had visions of him returning with a bottle of pop and a bag of crisps, however due to it being so cold the landlady allowed me in, how times have changed! (And by that I don't mean I'm barred from every pub in Nottingham! I'm referring to my age back then.) I remember it had an open log fire and was really warm and cosy. I still don't have a clue why we went to that pub a matter of two, if that, miles from home! I'm sure my Dad had his reasons!!! It was quite out of the blue, but strangely enjoyable. Anyhow, my lack of Flint-fix didn't hurt quite so much when I discovered on arriving home Mum had phoned the theatre concerned over the state of the weather and being told that the concert had indeed been cancelled.

A couple of weeks or so later I was in Math's class at school.... I'd better set this up.... I didn't like Math's at all. However I, along with best mate Karen really liked our teacher Mr. Robinson (aka 'Robbo'). We sat right in front of him at his desk for the last 3 years of our school life, and even though he wasn't what you'd call fanciable we sort of fancied him, as in a 'he's a lovely bloke' kind of way! I know, confusing isn't it, we were teenager's need I say more. Despite his dodgy dress sense and eye stinging aftershave, he was a fabulous teacher, great fun, and had it not been for his great personality and modern manner of teaching I'd never have passed my math's exams, so I thank you 'Robbo'! Anyhow, he'd got wind that the Flintlock concert had been cancelled in Mansfield a couple of weeks previous. How? I don't know, maybe a newspaper item perhaps? But it was due to things like this that made him the exceptional teacher he was. All the way thru this particular lesson he was so funny, with a naughty twinkle in his eye and his wicked sense of humour. He started off the lesson, and began...... "So, we've got this spotty drummer from this band and he's travelling at a speed of 50 miles per hour....................."etc. Soon after that "Right can anyone tell me, if you have a blond singer and a blond guitarist which one would be more likely to eat 19 apples and......................"etc. All perfectly reasonable Math's based questions but he would twist 'every' question to relate to 'the boys'. Although she wasn't a fan of the band she was my friend after all, and so Karen clicked what was going on and was in hysterics. I remember one of the boys in class saying "Sir, warra ya goin' on about". Mr. Robinson looked directly at me and with a real dead pan look on his face said "what does he mean Shelley"? I just looked wide eyed and kinda threw back a half smile coupled with a shrug. As the class drew to a close and everyone started to pack their things away, let's just say I had a few doodles on my pencil case. I was just about to put it in my bag when 'Robbo' walked by and just leaned on my desk and said "Mrs. Pascoe, just before you drift off into your own little world for dinner break could I trouble you to clean the black board". I was embarrassed, mortified and elated all at the same time. Going a nice shade of pink I walked towards the blackboard while everyone else was leaving the class. As I started to wipe the board 'Robbo' leaned on the wall, looked at me and said "When's the next one then Missy"? I said "Er, next what Sir"? in my shy little manner, no really, I was painfully shy at school. He said "the next Flintlock adventure". I smiled from ear to ear and said "Sunday Sir, going to Dagenham, can't wait" and I blushed again. He smiled (he had 'the' most lovely smile did 'Robbo') and said looking at Karen "I don't know, the quietest one in the class eh getting up to allsorts, who'd've thought it" he gave me another one of those cracking smile's and said "enjoy yourself trouble, go on the pair of ya then clear off"!!!! And with that Karen and I bumbled out of the class, Jacket's half on half off, bumping into door frames and giggling uncontrollably. Bless that teacher... 'Robbo'........Karen and I salute you.

On the subject of school, there was a class in English around this time where we had to write about 'My Weekend'........well, you don't need three guesses to know what I was going to write about. I handed in my assignment, and a few days later in the same class realized with horror my teacher Mrs. Appleton had given me 9 out of 10 for (her words) 'a silly spelling mistake on an otherwise different and refreshing subject'. My speeeling mistake apparently was that of Mike's surname....Holoway. She had corrected it with two 'L's. While she was a mighty fine teacher, she could be rather unapproachable now and again so I wrote underneath. 'Dear Mrs. Appleton it 'is' Holoway and not Holloway, he isn't the prison'. Where some teachers would've probably ripped into a student for being somewhat arrogant, as she gave books out during a class a week or so later she'd actually written underneath 'Apologies Shelley, after recent investigation I have discovered you're spelling is correct and apologies to Mr. Holoway'........ She then stood on one of the desks flapped her arms about and screeched like a parrot, and that is also true, we were half way through a drama class you see. Colourful teachers back then.

There was an occasion where the boys were doing a personal appearance (I think they may have performed a few numbers too) at The Palais in Nottingham........My Mum flatly refused allowing me to go. To be fair she did have a point, even though at

the time I could've won first prize for sulking, and tempting as it was I didn't slide down a wall crying either. The following day you see I had a dance exam at school so I did understand. I was just beside myself that 'they' were in Nottingham, and I couldn't see them. Oh the drama! So near and yet so flippin' far. As it happens I'd chatted to my dance teacher Mrs. Thompson about this the week before, and she was, as always very lovely and said "Never mind Shelley, it's all in a good cause and think how happy they will be for you when you pass your exam". 'Now there's faith' I thought. Anyhow, the Tuesday of the exam came and in front of some 'outside examiners', I did my bit to a piece of music called 'Pandora's Box'. After the exam I was sitting on the window ledge of the main hall (On the inside, eating my home made lunch…..not on the outside of the window, the exam hadn't gone that bad!)…and Mrs. Thompson walked up to me and sat at the side of me. "So, how did you feel it went Shelley", "I think it was OK, yeh" I said, hoping for the best outcome. "Well, they made the right noises about you so……fingers crossed lovie" she said…and then as she got up to walk away presented me with a little painted box (which I still have) inside the box there was a Flintlock badge! (yep, still have that too). She'd actually been down to the Palais the night before and from the merchandise stall or equivalent? purchased a badge for me, how kind was that. Oh and in case you were wondering………93%….pass, yay.
Some of these non-event-events were just as memorable as the real full-on-event-events!

Chapter Four... No Sex, No Drugs, Just Rock and Roll.

You know that generational thing where your Grandma would say things like "you don't know you're born, in my day........" Well, I'm about to do a bit of that now. But in the 1970's things 'were' different, and if you were 13, 14, 15, you were more inclined to be that actual age. Following the boys wasn't a sexual thing as such. Seriously, it was all about admiration, love, romance and the hopeless expectation of one of the boys being 'a boyfriend'. It all felt very 'safe'. Ok, so I can't speak for every single fan back then, but the girls I was associated with this was a fact. It was more Mills and Boon than Fifty Shades of Dagenham!

Flintlock had everything........including diverse personality's in the band........there was something for everyone. Well, that's how we 'the fans' saw it.

There was Mike......the cute one!
      Derek...the sax-y one!
      John......the friendly one!
      Jamie...the sensible one!
      And Bill..........the funny one!

It wouldn't surprise me even now if the boys hadn't realized this. But it was a fact this is how 'we girls' saw them.

Mike would always be the one circled and adored by swarms of girls.....Derek was the sweet one who could melt you with a simple 'hello'....John was always chatty, cheeky, and interested in what 'we'd' been up to and we quite liked that....Jamie was the man of reason, dignified and at times quite charming (with fabulous hair!)... and then there was Bill......oh Bill, he was the joker, great fun, and always had a witty one liner.

To be spoken to, acknowledged, remembered even, by any of the boys was soooo special. I remember the first time Mike said "arrhh you've come all the way from Nottingham haven't you". It was like winning some obscure prize! He'd remembered me! and

Nottingham!, arrrhhh. Another instance was Derek, signing an autograph for me on one of my many visits to Essex, writing my name without 'asking my name' and then to make it even better writing 'Shelley Welly'............awww, a few months on from that and more things to sign, Derek signed a photo of mine, 'To Shelley, Love Delly'........I was over the moon. One of the girls, Pauline, well her sir name back then was Tinker. Derek referred to her as 'Little Tink', she loved it, and why not. It's those little things isn't it that make memories special, plus they were nice guys it's as simple as that.

I had/have always been interested in music/performing, and one of the main reasons I liked this band, apart from the obvious was the music. I'd been influenced by my elder brother with regards to certain bands, The Beatles, The Who, The Small Faces, 10cc, etc, and by that I'm not complaining, he guided me wisely. I still like that music to this day. But I was seven years younger than my brother and well, 'Flintlock' were an outright choice of my own. I hadn't been led by my brother, friends, no one. I'd chosen to like them without the approval or introduction of anyone. I also liked the fact they played their own music too, quite a few bands around that time didn't. The boys however had got together via 'real life' and not some talent reality show route as many do today.

Meanwhile back in my own little world I'd adopted another new pen pal via the fans grapevine called Lou. After a couple of casual meets we arranged to go see the boys. I'd heard they were doing a gig of sorts at 'The Palais' Nightclub in Nottingham (although my parents referred to it as The Palais Dancehall). This was the second time the boys had been here and I wasn't going to miss them again. It was 'The Monday Phonograph' presents...208 Radio Luxembourg D.J. Tony Prince, plus a special appearance of Flintlock'. It was one of the times Mum was a little more at ease as it was a 15 minute bus ride away! I caught the 72 bus into town, which was 28p!!!... Once I'd arrived in town I walked down towards the Palais. I was so very proud they were in 'my' home town. I got off the bus and I kinda strutted my way down Upper Parliament Street, eat yer heart out John Travolta! It was a school night, so was done and dusted before 10.45pm! And although the band didn't perform what you would call a 'full on show', it was worth every penny of that 40p admission fee!!!! On meeting Lou we stood waiting outside, oh I had such butterflies, it was so exciting, I mean this was the first time I'd seen the boys on 'my' stomping ground. As we were allowed in I recognized a face, it was Tony Prince. I don't know why he was in the foyer of the club, meet and greet perhaps? He was really chatty and good fun with the fans creating a fabulous atmosphere, and as Lou and I got to the doors into the club he ushered us in and said "Precious cargo coming through, enjoy yourself girls". We squeaked back ever so over excited 'Thankyooooou" and there we were............in.

I remember lots of screaming girls (really!! ha ha) filling the dance floor area, it was pretty much full so we decided to stand on a slightly raised area, just a little to the side, close by the front on Bill's side of the stage. It's hard to describe how the excitement builds, it just did!!! The slightest change in lighting would have everyone going into a frenzy. Screaming was very popular this particular night, so as Tony walked out onto the stage the roof could've fallen in and you wouldn't have heard it! He did some chat and not so much warmed up as set the fans on fire, and all of a sudden there they were......our boys.......The girls went wild, I think fainting must've been in the fans contract that night also as within minutes someone was being carried out, then another, then another. As the band performed I seemed to be one of the very few who were actually singing along. I can see Bill now, looking over at me and smiling, and I 'know' he was thinking "Look at her, wow, singing along to our music, she is so

cool"................And then I wake up and realize his thought's may have been along the lines of "Great crowd, hope we can stop for something to eat on the way home, I'm starving".
I hadn't worn my Flintlock tee shirt etc for this particular occasion. I decided to 'dress up'. So along with my best jeans and a pink fluffy mohair jumper I wore 'Cachet' perfume and was very grown up indeed! Just reading up on that memory again, I can actually smell that perfume, how weird is that. Yes it was a very dignified evening, well for me. I behaved impeccably, unlike a few fans, who, let's say got slightly carried away. Here is a quote from the local Evening News the following day................................

'AT LAST NIGHT'S PALAIS 'MONDAY PHONOGRAPH EVENING', POP GROUP 'FLINTLOCK' ARRIVED ON STAGE LOOKING LIKE A MILLION DOLLARS, IN SUPER NEWLY AQUIRED SILK SHIRTS. THEY LEFT NOTTINGHAM IN NEWLY AQUIRED SILK TATTERS, AS SOME FANS TRIED TO CLAIM A LITTLE MORE THAN THEIR ENTRANCE TICKET ALLOWED'.

As soon as the show ended, and the lights went up I made my way out and went home. I know, yes you did read that correctly, me not waiting, unheard of. It wasn't as easy as I'm making it sound, but it was a school night. I'd promised Mum I'd go home directly after the show and I knew for a fact I'd be seeing them again.

So, I asked the girls to talk to me about their early memories of concerts and personal appearances............once the screaming had died down (hee hee) this is what they had to say.

"My first Flintlock concert was Hampton Wick, June 5th 1976. It was an afternoon fete followed by Flintlock in The Church Hall. Only a small gig but so lovely. I

stood next to John's Dad (who was the chief roadie!) and didn't realize who he was until I told him I was taking John home as he was mine, it was then he told me John was his son. Favourite song of the night was a cover of 'Can't Buy Me Love' (originally by The Beatles). Like Shelley's experience, the price of the ticket was an enormous 40p!!! I couldn't take any photos of the concert as I took so many in the day time I'd used up my film. Went home happy and on a different planet!"
…as told by Helen Morris

"With the help of my friend Val, we worked out that Sheffield City Hall was the first concert, May 1976. I loved the venue, still do. I have no idea how many fans were there, as I was concentrating on looking forwards to seeing the boys, and singing along to the songs, have never been a 'screamer' as such. My favourite song would have been 'I've Got My Eye On You' plus 'Flintlock…On The Way'. After the concert we met the boys outside and I feel sure the band 'Child' were there too, I have no idea why, just a memory flashback. I took a lot of photos of the concert, but not outside??? Maybe they never came out".
The other concert I remember, was the Scala Theatre in Rotherham. (I feel sure it was there). It was a Sunday concert, so helping as I usually did with the Sunday School, I had to make my excuses. Getting to the theatre, my friend Elizabeth ended up climbing up a drainpipe and getting in through a window. I stayed put and ended up getting a great unofficial meet and greet with the boys. Even then, it was meeting up with like-minded people, making new

friends and hearing other people's stories. The concert was amazing, as ever".
...as told by Lynne Brown

"Another memorable concert....Newcastle 18th October 1976....It was nice weather! I can't remember who I went there with, but the following year going back to same venue in Newcastle it started snowing the morning of traveling up there, fortunately it wasn't enough to stop the trains, or stop me! And I had a great time".
...as told by Helen Morris

'The first time I met the guys was at a signing in a record shop in Croydon. After that it was long rounds of Dagenham/gigs/TV and recording studios. I remember my best mate Gill wrote to 'Pink' magazine and asked if we could meet the band, they rang her and agreed. We went to the offices in London and were given amazing goodie bags with make-up, loads of singles, albums and other various pop goodies before being whisked away in a taxi. The guys were lovely and we had photo shoots with them and we felt like royalty ha ha. Can't remember what we chatted about but know there was a lot of fun and banter. Gill's granddad came to pick us up. I kissed Derek and then cried, oh the shame. They were only expecting a handful of people to turn up and it was packed out. They had to stop people coming in and then find a way of getting the boys out. Got to chat to them whilst getting stuff signed, it was quite a mad afternoon"!
...as told by Julyet Harris

"That record shop in Croydon is where the boys got mobbed and had to escape across the roof"!
…as told by June Sims

The New Vic concert from December '76 had been recorded by Capital Radio, and as I was in Nottingham and couldn't get that frequency on the radio, Lynne had recorded it and kindly done a copy for me on cassette. It was a potted version of the concert, to fit in with the radio timings I would imagine, but never-the-less still great to have……..and I still do! I may have ever so 'slightly' over played it after it originally reached me via the post all those years ago! It's evolvement from radio, to cassette tape, to CD, and finally to mini-disc in the hope of preserving it, did the job as it's still playable to this day. In fact close your eyes and you could be there. The absolutely deafening screams at the very beginning are worthy of any boy band then or now! In a world where the pop music business has changed so drastically, and technology has moved on so vastly over the decades since this recording, there is still one unchanged fact. Girls will be girls.
They opened with…………………..
Flintlock's….On The Way…… Followed by covers of songs by Peter Frampton, Steeley Dan, etc, peppered among their own songs………..
'Show Me The Way'
'Ricki Don't Lose That Number'
'Amorous Lady'
'My Love Is Not For Taking'
'Rocky Mountain Way'
'Route 66, rock and roll medley'
'Learn To Cry'
'Thunder Man'
'Pinball Wizard'

'Freeloader'
'Carry Me'
A little treasure I will always keep, and as it was my first ever concert, it is all the more special to have.

My favourite Flintlock song isn't actually listed here. So which song is it that can take me back to those days in an instant? 'Sea Of Flames'. There are actually two versions, both of which I love in equal measure. An organic version if you will, with just the boys, and an orchestrated one, written and arranged by Mike Batt, yes, he of the famous Wombles of Wimbledon. Beautiful melody and lyrics. For me it evokes very powerful memories from my flint-fan years. Also the cover version of The Beatles, 'She's Leaving Home', and the beautiful 'Taken All Away', are the three songs that instantly stand out for me, melody wise, and memories wise. These songs meant so much then, as they do still, and when I hear them now, it's like meeting up with old friends. Will never forget when I heard 'Russian Roulette' for the very first time, I thought it was a James Bond Theme....maybe it should have been.

Certain albums and particular songs meant different things to different fans............and the proof is here.

"For me, the album 'Hot From The Lock'...the boys recorded this on home ground, Wimbledon. So obviously the Wimbledon Gang we're all over it like a dirty rash. We went down to the studio to have a nosey and got more than we bargained for!!! We actually got hauled into the studio and ended up being recorded 'screaming' on the album! Not too intimidating then, us girls standing around a microphone screaming our heads off while the boys

looked on from the sound booth. We all got an 'F' necklace for doing that......and very sore throats"!
…as told by Lorraine Vickers-Bennett

"Hard choice and I loved them all - 'Taken All Away' has got to be my choice of single, I just love it. And 'She's Leaving Home'. With regard to the 'Hot From The Lock' album, Amanda, Lorraine and myself were also invited to re-scream for that - very difficult trying to scream to order over and over again - I remember screaming so hard I needed to wee! Still got the 'F' necklace we were given, but the sore throat is better. We all had such fun back then".
…as told by Helen Morris

"Oh it's so difficult to pin point a particular song, as I loved them all (love them all!!!) '……..On The Way' was just so exciting. I'm surprised my copy hasn't been worn out, the number of times I played it. There is so much to sing along with. 'Hot From The Lock' summed up 1976 for me, and this album was to be our only memory of Pauline's Quirkes until the DVD release all those years later. It also contains one of my favourite songs, 'I've Got My Eye On You'. The album 'Tears and Cheers', has my other favourite on, 'Russian Roulette', it is just so different and far removed from what was around back then and even now you'd never associate it with that typical 'boy band' tag. It's an amazing song, and I think on Facebook not too long ago someone was saying how it should be re-recorded. 'Russian Roulette came along at a time when we were all growing up along with our musical tastes".
…as told by Lynne Brown

"Oh gosh, I'm with Lynne on this one.......which one to pick? So I'm thinking, if I could only take one album with me onto a desert island, then it would have to be 'Hot From The Lock', best album from that balmy Summer of '76...'Carry Me'., sigh. The words mean so much to me. Thank you Flintlock, your beautiful music helped me more than you could ever imagine".
...as told by Pauline Vincent

'Carry Me' was always a favourite with the fans, and it was a beautiful ballad so it's perfectly understandable why it was so popular. It is also associated with the end of concerts, so it makes it a double whammy memory wise. I played it the other day after not hearing it for some time, and found myself singing word for word the whole song. Before it came out I'd already ordered a copy at a shop in Nottingham called 'Rediffusion'. This was the shop where all my Flintlock records were ordered and purchased from, each L.P., 'On The Way'........ 'Hot from the Lock', 'Tears and Cheers', 'Stand Alone', to all the singles, oh and the 12inch blue vinyl, 'Hey You, Your Like A Magnet'.
Rediffusion was a TV sales/rental shop upstairs and downstairs a record shop. A hallway led you past the TV showroom bit, towards a narrow staircase which in turn drew you down the stairs to a basement area where there were no windows just racks and racks of LP's, and smothered on the walls were posters of various bands and singers. The manager Les was a nice chap, he would listen to Linda and I rattling on about the boys each and every time we went in, which was often. There was also a cute assistant Steve, who would, without fail, wind us up about the boys whenever he was working and then very sweetly he'd play one of their records for us through the PA system in the shop while we took root at the counter. That place became a little social club for Linda and myself, it would be 'meet you at

Rediffusion', as opposed to 'meet you at the lions' (a phrase every Nottingham resident will know). By this time, at home I'd been banned from using the phone for all 'Flintlock related matters'. Friends could call in, but I couldn't call out, how was that fair? Anyhow this particular morning I needed to walk up to the phone box to call the shop and see if my record had arrived. I ventured up the hill to the top of Saxondale Drive, this was where I used to live, and it appeared I along with half the street needed to use the phone, grrrrrr. My phone call was 'of course' of the utmost importance, so it was frustrating to hear through the rattling windows of the phone box various people having mundane conversations about 'What did ya want from the shops again'? And 'So then she said to her, and then he said'....come on people, I'm waiting here. The wait in this case was worth it as getting through to the shop with my trusty 2p I was told, 'Yes, it's here for you to pick up', yippee. Within an hour I was on the bus travelling into town. And so the question is, 'Why is transport slower, when you need to get somewhere faster'? I eventually reached the shop, made my way downstairs, and there was greeted with some cheeky banter of "Oh is that the copy we accidentally dropped"? men, 'tut', so funny aren't they!

As Steve the assistant trotted off to get my record from 'out the back', I was lovingly looking at a picture of the boys on the wall. They were in their black tee-shirts with diamante musical notation on the front, all apart from Derek that is. His had wording in a heart that read 'Kiss Me'…………….and breath.

The assistant returned and teased with the 'you can have it, you can't have it' game over the counter. Eventually it was in my hands. The thrill of getting a record back then was so satisfying. The picture detail to the wording, and then the excitement of finding out what the 'B' side was called. Sometimes the inner sleeve also had a picture on it. Something I have missed in recent years. With 'Carry Me' safely in my paws I observed the sleeve.

This colour picture sleeve was a treat in itself, all the boys in red 'Flintlock' sweatshirts. Umm, yeh...... It doesn't sound so good that does it, but it was ok actually. When the single was released, there was a token on the back of the sleeve. HA......Can't get that with a 'download' can you! And the idea was you cut it out and send in the token, as proof that you'd purchased the record, and I think there was one of those 'In no more than 15 words say why....................bla bla', to a competition address, which I believe was Pinnacle Records (the bands record label). The prize was to spend the day with Flintlock. I didn't win, and cue the violins. Actually none of my girlies won it (more violins, we need more violins)! While it would have been very nice indeed to win our failure to didn't upset us too much. In fact there was no feeling of loss really, with our now regular trips down to Essex and a diary full of impending concert treats............the future was looking Flintlockingly bright.

Chapter Five... Carrier Bags + Lip Gloss = Dagenham!

Dagenham, Dagenham, Dagenham!.........it was our 'Mecca'. This was the place where the boys came from and where we went to! Yes, most Sunday's to be exact, sometimes mid-week if it was the holidays. We would arrive midday and then stroll the streets going to and from each of the boys homes, hoping to see them, speak to them, have photos taken with them. More often than not, we were lucky in that, we did. We must have walked miles. Over time when I've looked back and I put myself in the shoes of the boy's families and their neighbours. Oh dear, how patient were they with us. Most times actually, on very odd occasions not! And we would now and again get an ear bashing of 'keep the noise down', from irate neighbours just wanting a quiet Sunday afternoon. You can't blame them really. Sorry about that............ sincerely I am. While I don't recall ever being 'noisy' as in rowdy and rude, the 'noise' in our case was possibly over excited chat, giggling, and the odd yelp if any of the boys actually came to their front doors. This was of course in the early days of visiting........As the months went on we mellowed in our approach to 'waiting' outside the houses. It seemed soon after the boys became well known, Mike's family up sticks and left the area for Chelmsford, I don't know if that was due to the band situation or something they had previously planned. We would always make our first port of call Calverley Crescent which was where Derek lived. I even persuaded fave cousin Debbie (aka 'Cuz Deb') to come to Dagenham once. I say persuaded as she was one of 'Donny's girls' you see! However she succumb to my pestering and on arriving and heading towards Derek's house, she huffed "Huh, I don't really know why I came, I mean it's not like I......OHH, OOOOWW THERE HE IS, THERE'S DEREK, HE'S JUST COME OUT OF THAT HOUSE". So all in all, I think the trip down to Essex had the desired effect. Just around the corner from

Derek's as the crow flies was Bill's home, and down the road John's, and a little further on Jamie's place, so it was the obvious meeting point. Outside Derek's house was a grass verge and we would meet there, sit, and wait. Actually thinking back, from '76 to '79 so many of us stood/sat there so often it's a wonder that grass managed to grow at all! We went armed with sandwiches, drinks and I even had a teeny tiny radio, covered by a teeny tiny leather cover! Hence, why, whenever I hear Gerry Rafferty's 'Baker Street' it takes me right back to sunny Sunday visits, as it always seemed to be played on the radio whilst visiting Dagenham. I know flinty friend Ann will agree with me on this, even now we text each other if it's a sunny day and we hear 'Baker Street' on the old wireless. Happy day's indeed. No mobile phones, so how were we able to let each other know what time we'd arrived, left, and more importantly which direction we'd gone in! Well, believe it or not, chalk! Yes, we would leave each other chalked messages or black felt pen scribbles on the lamp post outside Derek's house. Mobile phones! Mobile-Schmobile pah! The other rather extravagant means of finding out such information was, firstly finding a phone box to phone your parents, beforehand however instructing your Mum to call someone else's Mum at a certain time, to link up that way!!! Although my Mum for one got fed up with that idea pretty early on, so it wasn't as popular as the tried and tested chalk/pen method! Plus, chalk didn't tell you off for wasting it's time!
I'm not sure how, but within my little circle of girls I always seemed to get voted to knock on Derek's door. Yehhhh, thanks for that girls!!! "You do it, no you do it" was the regular banter, but I usually did it. You see his Dad could be stern, although I have to say on the 'one' occasion 'he' did open the door to me, he was nice enough. Never underestimate the power of the sweet smile, polite manners, head tilt approach. Bill's Mum was always a delight, as were John's family. To say they must've had their

door knocked at, at least two dozen times each Sunday, they certainly dealt with that fiasco with patience and grace. Not so sure I could have. I even peer through the letter box first when 'friends' call at my house! But seriously it wasn't like a month's worth, this was over three years at the least that these families tolerated the fans. By the time we got to Jamie's place we'd usually walked off so much energy, and chatted for England, we were a little more subdued.

While I have no idea how we all found out where the boys lived, we just did. Well, there were certain means, not illegal you understand, just cheeky, sneaky perhaps. At the very worst I'm talking tactics that would have been, let's say frowned upon! (....mainly by our parents actually). We'd have made rather good detectives. Without the help of the 'still to be invented' internet we found out, addresses, which hotels the boys were staying at, studio locations, flight's at the airport, you name it, we found it. Anyhow, after a couple of initial visits it was the most natural thing to just 'pop down to Dagenham' for the day! I was usually with Linda and/or Viv on these trips, now and again with Jane, and high days and holidays a small group of us, sometimes picking up our Leicester friends, Ros, Carole, Ali and Bev via the train journey en route. There were times when we'd pre-arrange to meet fellow fans, and other times just 'turn up'. I once went down on my own! I can't believe I did that! But the thing was I was confident that once I'd got there, I'd meet up with someone I knew, and I did. That's something I wouldn't have the nerve to do now, Flintlock wouldn't be there anyhow! Ah ha!

I met some lovely 'flinty-fans' in Dagenham as the diaries suggest.

"Me, Viv and Jane get to Dagenham and don't really recognize anyone except for these two girls I met once before Ann and June (or Jane?). Ann said she'd seen Mike and he'd said 'hello', he was in

Derek's house. We stood chatting and Ann shared a packet of biscuits with us, that was nice of her. Then Sandra – Derek's sister – came out to post a letter and said hello. Later on we bumped into Tina and Julia, the girls from Luton. They are the girls I met them at Dagenham last month and we have started writing to each other. Then this girl called Jackie we'd met the week before came running over the road to us right happy to see us and said she'd seen Derek that morning and he promised he'd come out to talk to us in the afternoon".

We always had bags and bags of 'stuff' with us! I don't think in the history of 'flintlock', did I ever visit Dagenham without having a carrier bag full of 'stuff'. It used to tickle me how groups of us would pass on either side of the road, all armed with our carrier bags, full of, I would imagine, similar things! Sandwich and a drink. *tick* Various 'stuff' for the boys to sign. Album sleeves, magazines, photos, autograph book! *tick* Camera. *tick* Gift's for the boys. *tick* Brush for windswept hair. *tick* and last, but not least, lip gloss. *tick* Yes, on the train from London to Dagenham Heathway, the 'group' lip gloss would do it's rounds, to ensure we all looked as glam as lip glossin' possible.

If only there were more Dagenham related tales…..and as if by magic……….

"Somehow I ended up finding out where they lived, and I think it took me two and a half hours to get from Dartford to Dagenham by public transport! I couldn't go as much as I wanted as my other passion at the time was dance, and on Saturday's it was theatre workshop and extra ballet, pointe work. I saw them as often as I could though. Due to the dancing side of my life I also met one of Derek's sister's,

Gaynor, at a dance festival. She saw my Derek badge on my dance bag and we became pen pals for just over a year or two".
…as told by Pauline Vincent

"Oh Dagenham days….if Bill wasn't in his Mum or his brother Rodney would always take the time to have a chat, so would John's Mum and Dad, they were so nice. This next bit is directly out of my diary from back then."…………………'Went to Dag, me and June got a curry and I love Mike'!!!
…as told by Ann French

"Ann and I used to use our season tickets to get to London and when we went to Dagenham we then used to get half price (child fare) on the bus"!
…as told by June Sims

"I still go into hysterics when I recall this story. Being one of four and having to use most of my money on magazine's and records, desperate measures were needed to get me to Dagenham. A girl at school put Elizabeth and me forwards for a job collecting charity pools coupons and money! Not sure how legit it actually was even back then, but hey, it was the school holidays and so we set off early. The only down side was we had to catch two buses to get there and it was snowing, really deep Sheffield snow! We managed to get round most houses during the day, but we did have to return at night. Our final collection was proving tricky. We could see and hear the people were in but they were not answering the front door. The only option was to try around the back. The only thing that was illuminating our way round was the snow, but we were determined. Elizabeth went first. She had only taken a few steps when SPLASH! Yep, she had gone straight into the garden pond and had taken the money with her. Instead of helping her out, I was beside myself, with tears rolling down my face. We managed to get most of the money out, but then left. Goodness knows what the householders thought when they saw their disheveled garden in the morning! The final straw of the whole episode was getting home. We managed to find a payphone and arranged for Elizabeth's Dad to pick us up from town, but we did have one soggy bus ride to get there. I'm surprised the driver let us on the bus in the first place, we were soaked. After that there was no more pools collecting. We went for the safe option and got a paper round. All this just to gather the money together to go to Dagenham"!

"I have to say though that aside most of our actual journey's down to Dagenham were pretty uneventful travel wise. On such a trip I had my first experience of a Harrods sale. The overwhelming memory was crashing and smashing crockery! I came out with a can of 7Up and a Harrods carrier bag"!

…as told by Lynne Brown

"When we met Derek at his house on August 21st we asked him what he thought about Elvis dying and Derek said 'he was a great guy'. Later on he asked me and Carole how much it cost us on the train from Leicester to London and we said £3.55, Derek said 'that's not bad'. We showed him an article in 'Pink' magazine which said 'Flintlock' were too well groomed, like mummies boys and should go more punk rock". Someone asked Derek if he had a good time in Japan. Derek said 'yes, had a great time, even though it rained and he had wanted to bring one of the waitresses home in his suitcase'! As we stood chatting to him we asked him what he'd been doing all morning and he said painting his bedroom black. Then we asked him where his bedroom was and he said 'front of the house on the left'. We later walked down to see John. Sadly he wasn't in, but his sister chatted to us for a while and even showed us some photographs of the band. We then walked to Jamie's house. He was also out, so we had a chat to his sister Ruth".

"I loved the trips down to Dagenham. Just looking through my old diary I notice one August going down on mass, Me, Carole, Helen, Chris, Lynn, Karen, Lorraine, Amanda, Debbie, Sharon, about 13 of us in all, great day. At a later date in the year, after visiting Pinnacle Records we went to Dagenham. Felt lucky as Derek was in and he answered the door to us and chatted for about half an hour, and he wrote in my autograph book 'Help, I have been captured by three girls from Leicester'…We then went down to Jamie's and while we stood talking to Jamie, Bill arrived in his car to borrow some car ramps. We were all talking about the rock group 'Uriah Heap'. Then we went to John's and joking about this and that. Then we had to leave to get home and John told us a quicker way to get to Dagenham Heathway".

…as told by Alison Grey

The magazines were full of Flintlock at this time, most in favour, and some, not so much. But, if we all liked the same things, what a boring world we would live in. The odd piece of negativity would upset me though. This was my lovely little world, full of 'nice', how dare anyone try and spoil that .Back then it was a popular thing to have questionnaires in the teenage magazines, asking pop groups the obvious things like, 'What's your favourite colour', and 'What's your favourite food'. It allowed us to get to know our boy bands a little better, even though back then, they were just called 'groups'! The 'bands' reference soon followed.....and the 'boy' bit was introduced a few years later, how that's never been a question on Mastermind is baffling. Chatting to the 'chaps' about these questionnaires I do remember Bill saying of a particular article however, "I had flu, they didn't even get the chance to ask me so all these answers are made up", umm defeating the object there somewhat. However, while we would still collect the magazine offerings, Linda and I put our own questionnaires together for the boys to complete. Among some of our more obvious questions we had 'What colour underpants do you have on'? (Oh we were so full of confidence)......'What is your motto in life'? And 'What do you dislike about being in the public eye'? Thankfully not one of our five sweethearts ever wrote 'the fans'. My personal favourite was 'If you could change one thing right now, what would it be'? On a visit to Dagenham we managed to see three of the boys and got said questionnaires filled in. It was a midweek visit and fortunately for us, was one of those days where it was Linda and I, and the boys, on a one-to-two basis, yeeeeee (that was me yee-ing). These times for any fan were extremely few and far between so we made the most of it and the questionnaires were a great source of entertainment for both parties. We were able to leisurely enjoy their company. Yeh, felt very spoilt that day. We decided to go to Bill's house first ....We asked if he minded filling in the questionnaire, "Course not, give it here then". He then went into what seemed a half an hour cabaret spot. Perfect. Who knew that little questionnaire would bring us so much joy. He said that the thing he didn't like about being in the public eye was "Not being able to walk down to the shops without hordes of gorgeous scantily clad women throwing themselves at him"………Okaaayy. Then he reached the question 'What is your motto in life', he replied whilst writing "Well it used to be, 'Don't Let 'Em Grind You Down', but after this it's "Always Send Ya Mum To The Front Door In case There Are Strange Women With Questionnaires"….we loved it, 'women' indeed!!! Before long he was at the final question, 'If you could change one thing right now, what would it be'?………He wrote, "To be able to travel back in time and read this questionnaire properly before I began to fill it in". Ya gotta love Bill, and we did.

Later on at Derek's, once again the questionnaire was greeted with intrigue, "What colour underpa………………oh, I see, like that is it", he said, and I remember blushing! It was easily done back then. The answer came back "Black, er I think"? and then he gestured as if to check. Giggle sniggle. After the dissection of said questions, he finally reached the question. If you could change one thing right now, what would it be? He answered, "Probably to live next door to you (looking at me) so you didn't have a long journey to face"…….he was smooth, definitely smooth, I'll give him that. I was on cloud nine. Linda joined in with "Owwwwww Shelley, owwww, that is soooo sweet, awwwww" and kept nudging me whilst giggling………and I blushed again…………and again…..and……let's just say I looked healthy that day. Soon after completion of form we said our goodbyes, received hugs and kisses and made our way to Johns…….he wasn't home…nooooooo. Here is my diary account of that………..Quote…

"We walked to John's……….. he wasn't in"

…….. It's hard to know how to follow that, and I have to admit on finding this nugget of information recently in one of the diaries, I went into uncontrollable laughter. It may look rather strange to log such information looking at it now, but at the time, it was seriously important. So much so, I'd actually drawn two little tears at the side of it, awwww. We did however manage to get hold of Jamie, wa-hey! And he filled in the questionnaire as requested. He started reading and suddenly burst out "Errmm, red", "Eh"? We replied, "Underpants, red underpants"………..and he carried on filling in the questionnaire as if completing an important exam. We discovered Jamie's dislike of being in the public eye was 'big heads and show offs'? Still not sure if he read that one correctly. It came to '………..if you could, change one thing right now……bit. He tapped his pen on his chin and wrote 'To be performing in a concert', Linda said laughing "Is that as opposed to standing here chatting to us hee hee"? "Oh no, no, not at all" he said "but if I was doing a concert, let's face it, chances are you two would be there wouldn't you, you must spend a fortune, your pretty much at 80% of them"…..and we both gushed at the acknowledgement that Jamie recognized us. Man of few words ya see, so it meant a lot.

He was correct as it happens, we did go to a lot of concerts and appearances, oh and Dagenham – how could I forget that - and yes, admitted, spend a small fortune in doing so, but as my Mum explained once to a narky neighbour who said to her in passing conversation, "Oww I think it's unhealthy a young girl like your Shelley being so obsessed with a group"……….Mum soon put her in her place, "Er exc---use me" she said, "It's nice for her to have the boys as an interest, and she has lovely friends because of it. Besides, it's a damned sight better than your Pat getting up to goodness knows what on Vernon Park at all hours". She left the poor woman standing there open mouthed. As Mother did an about turn she huffed, "Hu, the cheek of it, 'she' needn't start getting all hoytie toytie with me", and with that my Mum waltzed off, head held high, with me in tow trying to keep up with her confident stride.

After this particular Dagenham visit, we 'just' managed to get our train back to Nottingham. We'd traveled down so many times, it was getting to the point where some of the rail staff were recognizing us, hence why we still got our train as we were noticed racing through the station, carrier bags flapping behind us whilst shouting, "hold the train", and they did. Travelling back home that evening with a wealth of memories as the train took us north, I scribbled all those memories in my diary so I wouldn't forget a single thing, and here I am, writing about it……so it worked didn't it.

Chapter Six... No More Waiting or Anticipating, '77 Tour.

When the tour dates were announced for the '77 tour it was my one aim in life to go to as many as I possibly could. I pleaded with my Dad to do a 'car boot' so that I could raise some money selling things I no longer wanted. Fortunately I was one of those kids that looked after their stuff, so my games, no longer fitting clothes and 'Pippa' dolls I'd grown out of and various other bits and bobs all went in the sale. We did a car boot one very cold Sunday morning in Calverton, thankfully it paid off as it covered two thirds of the cost of concert tickets, travel expenses and B&B accommodation. The rest was accumulated by saving every penny of pocket money and doing odd jobs, taking the empties back to the 'Beer-off' (which you might know as the 'Off Licence') for the 2p return on the bottle, baby sitting and the like.

It was like a military operation, I mean apart from actually 'doing' the gigs, 'we were' touring! Again, I don't recall all the intricate details of how we organized all this. I just remember getting it done, with some help from Mum of course. On her advice I did go to the local library and found a book on hotels and B&Bs in the U.K., and I must've sat for 3-4 hours writing down addresses and phone numbers. You see I was in charge of 'where to stay'. Sometimes just a case of staying at each other's homes. It was a little complicated here and there in that, depending on the concert, area of the country, there may be two of us, sometimes three, four, or there could be a whole group of us. Yes I 'spose the cost was rather high, well, not as today's prices go, but when you compare it to my weekly pocket money allowance that is! It didn't seem to matter though, if it ticked the box of 'close to the concert hall' then more often than not that is where we would stay.

My birthday of this particular year was dedicated to all things 'Flintlock'! Well done that Mother. One of my gifts was a package of two photo albums with two films for my camera, and two boxes of flashbulbs. Everyone now has cameras in their phones, it's so easy. You just see something and take your phone out to take a photo. Then you can check it on your phone, and if you don't like it delete it. Back then you had to have your camera with you if you wanted photos. Then once the film was finished you did one of two things. You'd either send the film away to be developed. Or you'd take it to a photo shop/Boots for example (other shops available!) to get your film developed. Oh the excitement of going to pick up your photos, I think possibly it was on an equal par of going to buy a record. I'd lovingly take them out of the folder, holding by the edges so that I didn't get finger prints on them. Sometimes you'd take 31 photos with your camera at a concert and then have a few odd frames left to fill up the film of 36 when you got home. So I would take photos of the dog, the garden, the dog in the garden, anything, just so long as I could get that film in to be developed. It was great when the photo companies started to do developing with two smaller duplicate photos at the side of the photo. It meant you could share with your friends/pen pals. The birthday package didn't end there, I was also given a carpet bag for travelling, and travel hair dryer. I still have the carpet bag! I've used it many, many times, it was obviously made very well. If that bag could talk!.................Ummm, I'd probably be working in a circus!
The gifts were useful and so welcome, anything that could save a bit of money during the tour time.
I'm ashamed to say, my one and only 'naughty', was one time travelling to London on the train (only one way, my nerves couldn't have coped with two directions) and from getting on the train, I stayed in the toilet so that I didn't have to buy a ticket. *hangs head in shame* Now that's grim. What possessed me?

Lack of money, that's what. The cover story for people wanting to use the loo was 'severe travel sickness'. When we reached London and got off the train (Lou was in a toilet further down the train you see...there's a joke there!)...I felt sick, oh the irony! I had our back up story of "oh no, I'm so sorry I must've dropped them as we were getting off the train" all ready and rehearsed in my head, but I still felt really sick. 'This' for me, was very out of character, but this was a desperate measure to get to the gig, and not for one minute am I bragging about this, it was awful, just awful. We got closer to the guard, knowing he would be asking for tickets at the end of the platform, and I began to feel even sicker, I started sweating and felt light headed. Then, as if by magic, we must have been three people away from him, he just decided to move to the side of the gate and waved us all through. Uh? We couldn't believe it. We were thrilled. Thrilled we hadn't been caught red handed and thrilled the guard was having an off day. So thrilled in fact that my nerves had a field day, I found the nearest public convenience and let's just say I lived up to my sickly feeling! A little later as Lou was getting us a coffee, I called my Mum up from the station to let her know we'd reached London and like a complete idiot told her what I'd just done. I think I must've been experiencing that whole 'confessional' thing. She just said "What a stupid thing to do our Shelley, I'm not surprised you've been ill, I should imagine you won't be so silly on the way home". And I whimpered, "No Mum". Ah, so much for the sympathy vote.

Yes 1977, this was the most fantastic year............... Flintlock were busy busy, and 'busy busy' meant so were we! I can't comment on every show I was lucky enough to see as I don't think there is enough paper available in WH Smiths to permit that. But I will however share one or two rather memorable concerts. So, in no particular order.

October 27th, Leicester De Montfort Hall. This was a great show, and a great location. Not too far away from home, and we knew we would be seeing friends at this venue. We had previously reserved our tickets over the phone, so Linda and I made an early start to get to Leicester and pick up said tickets. Firstly after getting off the train, we walked a very short distance to our B&B we'd booked in for the night, it was nice, clean, friendly, and more importantly, a steal at £5.00 each! Walking to the theatre we stopped off to buy an orange carnation for Mike, and a red rose for Derek. We arrived at the theatre got our tickets and then mingled with some 'other' fans. This wasn't an exclusive Flintlock concert, but they were headlining it. Sheer Elegance, 60's band The Love Affair and Guys and Dolls were also on the bill. We'd managed to get Row B. at £2.50 each, seats 26 and 27, so good position. Once we had the tickets safely in hand, we went down to Radio Leicester where we knew the boys were going to do a radio interview regarding the concert. There we met Tina, Julia and Bev. Then some other fans we knew arrived from London called Andrea, Janet and Chris. Very soon after this Newton turned up with Derek and John. The excitement with only a few of us was ridiculous really, but it just was soooo exciting. We took photos, received welcome hugs from John and Derek, and then the boys went in to do the interview. Before going in Linda asked Newton where the rest of the boys were, "they're up at De Montfort Hall" back came the reply………so……..back went Linda and I to the venue leaving the others at the radio station. So much walking, always walking, I was so fit back then. Linda wanted to get there because of Mike arriving, and I'd had my Derek hug so all was well in the world. Anyhow on arriving back at the venue, we walked past these sliding glass doors and they just opened, then everything seemed to happen so quickly, Linda dived in and they closed again. I saw a steward (or the like) running after her and she was last seen disappearing down a corridor. It was so comical. I wandered around outside the building for a while, rather aimlessly, not knowing what to do really, and then heard these voices that sounded familiar coming from an open window on the first floor, which drew me a little closer. There I am looking up at the building thinking 'Ummm, what do I do now'?........ "You should get in through that window" said a voice behind me, and I turned around to see these two Guys and Dolls fans – looking every bit like their idols in white suits, red shirts and red 'button hole' carnations – "Do you think so"? I said. I explained about Linda getting in, and then one of the girls who I later got to know as Janet said "listen, we've been here almost two hours now and the only ones that have arrived are some of 'your lot', Flintlock yeh, and another band, they went in about 40 minutes ago, and that's them you can hear talking. They've just been cheeky with us having a laugh, shouting things out of the window". Anyhow on deciding whether or not to actually climb through this downstairs toilet window, I suddenly found myself being levered through it with the help of the Guys and Dolls fans. I was in! While I was there, I nipped to the loo (like you do).........and then I ventured into the corridor. It was reasonably quiet. I could vaguely hear people talking in various rooms. My heart was beating so fast and so loud too, and my hands had gone all sweaty, I was in, but not exactly sure what to do next. Then this youth walked by me all dressed in black – not a Goth – nothing along those lines really back then, I figured he was a stage hand. He looked at me, I looked at him, and he said "Alright". I nodded. He carried on "You looking for the band". I nodded again. He then quite politely led me up the stairs by instructing "follow me", which I did. We were soon up a flight of stairs and he knocked on the door of the first room "there you go" he said, and just left me standing there. The door opened and..............................Eh? That wasn't Flintlock. It was a band, but not mine. The Love Affair seemed quite friendly though. In a strange twist of fate later on in life when I became an entertainment manager in Scarborough in the early 1990's, I did actually employ the Love Affair for a 60's themed weekend. Would've thought it, I know I certainly wouldn't back then.

On leaving the doorway I was aware my name was being shouted like a racing car whizzing by, it was little Linda, still being chased by security! She was laughing like a crazy woman as well as charging towards me, her excited whoops and eeeeks were echoing around the corridor, and at that moment as she was within a few feet of me, the door to the opposite dressing room opened and Big Mick (Mikes Dad and Flintlocks manager) stood there. "What on earth is going on out here" he said. Linda had reached me by now, as had the security man, red faced and a bit miffed. "It's alright mate" said Big Mick towards the security man, "We know these two" then carried on "you're not 'sposed to be in here you know". We did know this, but what is a girl to do, the heart wants what the heart wants. We were craning our necks trying to get a glimpse inside the dressing room as the door softly closed behind him. "Right then you pair come with me". We thought he was leading us outside but he took us through to the wings and then……… into the auditorium….whoop. "Sit there and behave" he instructed…….so we did, and pretty soon after the boys walked out on stage to do their sound check (*controls urge to scream*).

Wow, what a fabulous treat. Although they did a little more than this, I do remember them sound checking to 'Thunder Man' and a little of 'Learn To Cry', there was some sound feedback here and there and so the sound guys were sorting out the problems. During all this Derek walked to the front of the stage, rather bemused at seeing us sitting there, he shielded his eyes from the stage lights until he'd focused on us both and then just pointed to us. We both waved, and giggled, and he called "What you up to sitting there". I joked at how I was their new manager, and he called back "OK, cool". Personally I found that experience watching the sound check as interesting as the actual show. As it came to a close, we decided, without prompt, to go back outside (must've started to mature a little!)................and with that waved to the boys. Derek walked over to the edge of the stage with John and said smiling "Oh so you're not on backing vocals tonight then"? "I wish" was my instant reply. Little did I know what my future had instore.

'De Montfort Hall' doesn't have the highest stage and so they both knelt down and gave us a kiss, and then I passed the rose to Derek. Honestly, the ticket price had already surpassed itself at that point. Do people still say 'swoon'?............'Ahhhhh swoon'.

We then went outside only to meet up with even more familiar faces, some of which were the Leicester girls, Carole and Ali. There was a great atmosphere outside, lots of chants and singing occurring. It was friendly, exciting, and within a couple of minutes of being back in the cold the two 'Guys and Dolls' fans who'd very kindly shoved me through the open window suddenly rushed over to hear about our indoor adventure. Nice girls I remember, a little older than us, their names were Janet and Karen, and when we compared tickets we discovered Linda and I were sitting 'directly' behind them, now that was strange! Eventually we were allowed in and there was an exciting rumble of walking/chatter/laughter..........It was a very mixed age group audience I recall, but it was a very mixed show so..............Once in there we were all scuffling in our bags for cameras only to be told "Sorry you can't use that in here" by stewards, so that marred things a tad. However, one thing that did cheer us up were our Guys and Dolls fans in front of us, turning around chatting and suddenly saying "Listen girls 'Guys and Dolls' close the first half, so why don't we swap seats in the interval so that you can be on the front row when Flintlock come on". How thoughtful of them. Of course we took up their kind offer.

The show started and 'Sheer Elegance' walked out living up to their name. 'Love Affair' followed soon after and had us all waving our arms and singing along, then 'Guys and Dolls' came on to do a spot and close the first half of the show. Well at that time in my life, they wouldn't have been on my record play list. However they did a very polished performance, looked every inch the professionals, and their harmonies sounded nice. So in honour of our new friends, and respect to the act I sang along, and generally had quite a pleasant time. I have to say, if I hear them played on the radio now I think fondly of our brief 'moment in time' together and meeting Janet and Karen. They were lovely girls and I hope they both went on to have happy lives.

In the interval we, as arranged, swapped places with the girls and then before we knew it our time arrived. With the stage set the boys walked out onto the stage to hysteria and deafening screams. Even Janet and Karen were cheering behind us, and I remember really liking that. The songs we'd heard at the sound check were now heading towards us in all their glory. It was fabulous. Soon into the concert, some familiar faces rushed down to the front, security were throwing themselves about as if they were saving footballs coming towards a goal. Before we knew it, the girls were up on the stage. One of those girls being 'Grace from Biiiiirrrmmminggggham'!....Save yourself Mike, save yourself!

Here are a few personal memories from Ali's diary.

"Carole and I arrived and went around to the stage door and met fans from Luton and Nottingham. Newton was selling merchandise inside and he tried to sell me a photo of Mike and I told him I didn't like Mike! They sang, Flintlock's On The Way, My Love Is Not For Taking, Ricki Don't Lose That Number,

Thunder Man, Learn To Cry and various others including a new one, 'Anything For You'. They were all wearing tight black trousers! Grace and Marie climbed up onto the stage 3 times! During 'Thunder Man' there was dry ice and Grace climbed on stage, dodged a bouncer and hid behind the amplifier and during all the smoke, she dragged Mike off his drum kit and onto the floor (go Grace!) which threw Derek, causing him to forget the words to the song".
…as told by Alison Grey

Yes, I believe that was a record even for Grace that night, three times up on the stage in one concert. During the Rock and Roll Medley the boys gestured to the audience to get up and dance, we didn't need telling twice and the 'Guys and Dolls' fan's got up dancing too. In fact most of the audience we're up on their feet dancing. This was such an enjoyable night for a whole host of reasons, a different feel to the regular concerts, almost a party. Once again and way too soon the first few bars of 'Carry Me' started and so did the sinking feeling in my tummy. I stood there singing and swaying, just avoiding being bopped on the head with the over excited arm waver at the side of me, thinking "One day, yeh, I'm going to do that" looking up at the stage. I had a love/hate relationship with that song, loved the song, hated the fact it meant end of show time.

"…I love Flintlock, I just hate it when I hear Carry Me 'cos I know they are finishing the show…..the girl at the side of me crackin' me up singin' all the wrong words hee hee, dead funny………"

Unlike the girl at the side of me I was singing the correct lyrics to 'Carry Me'……..hers, well, they left a lot to be desired…..In a rather high pitch I could hear………

............."Carry Me, help me find today, Carry Me, don't rake the band away"..........ahhh such touching lyrics, gets ya right there! The little brunette was at the concert on her own, and bless her heart, tried to take a 'selfie' during the last number. Back then it was just called a 'Struggling to take a photo of yourself whilst holding the flash down at the same time'ie'. So I offered my services and took a quick pic of her with the boys/stage in the background. We were rather smothered in fan-oflauge by that time so the stewards had no way of stopping us, let alone getting anywhere near us. I wonder if the little brunette still has that photograph?

The concert finished and the lights went up. Our new 'friends' Janet and Karen said how we'd made their day! And how they'd had a terrific time, so once again as we tended to at these shows, addresses and phone numbers we exchanged, and I promised them, if the boys did anything Nottingham wise I'd let them know", which a short time later I did. Many people had already left the auditorium, and as we put our jackets on, I have no idea what possessed us to do it but Linda and I jumped up onto the stage, ran through the wings and got backstage............and we were instantly thrown out again. Ha ha ha........but it was fun and it did make us laugh. We laughed such a lot in those days. On getting outside and mingling with our friends and fellow fans, I decided to get a chant-sing-song going, which proved popular. Then Big Mick came out and black mailed, ha YES! Black mailed us into behaving, so the boys could get out of the building to the relative safety of the car. The deal was if we allowed them to get out safely, they would sign autographs for five minutes. Seemed like a good deal. As they came out of the stage door Linda raced towards and then clung to Mike like a leech, I leaned in and got a kiss from Mike, and then one from Linda!!! Then I received my third hug of the day from Derek just before he got into the car. The boys looked really happy and

were in high spirits, I'm thinking possibly from the concert buzz. They did sign a few autographs within the safety of the car, it was the only occasion I ever got 'me' signed, as in on my arm, but within 5 minutes as arranged they were leaving. Grace, Marie, and a girl called Sue ran after the car along with a few others. We decided against that, and then for our little journey due to the chill in the air we got a taxi back to the comfort of our B&B, which tells me the following day we must have been going south not to have gone home. My feet were absolutely killing me, but it had been worth it. Once back in our new 'home' for the evening I starred lovingly at my newly signed arm and we sat and chatted into the wee small hours about our very eventful, fun filled day. Did we 'ever' sleep?
…….and here's Ali again with more diary snippets, followed with some of the girls' memory flash backs.

Afterwards we all went round to the stage door again and shouted things up to their dressing room. Someone started off the singing and chant, as in "Give us an F"….and we all shouted 'F', "Give us an L"…'L', Give us an "I"…'I', and so on, until it spelt out Flintlock. Bill then came out onto the staircase and was swinging on the staircase like a gorilla! At 11pm Big Mick came down to talk to us and said if we let the guys get into the car he would let them sign autographs for 5 minutes. So they did and signed autographs for us".
…as told by Alison Grey

"It's amazing how the memories linger about this time. I had only just started work when the '77 tour dates were announced, so I booked my holidays to coincide. After giving my Mum money for my keep

and the money for my bus fares to Dagenham nearly every night, I saved every last penny towards the tour. Mum helped me book B&B's near each venue, apart from a couple of times where I managed to stay with Pen-friends. It was great meeting up with so many lovely friends".

"I only missed the 8th April concert, I think it was Hull? The first one on 4th April was Caird Hall, Dundee where the front row collapsed on my legs. Was I worried about my legs? Oh no, I was worried about my photos that I had taken with me and my camera. At the Glasgow City Hall gig the following night I was allowed to sit upstairs at the side of the stage instead of front row as I was still a bit shaken up".
…as told by Helen Morris

"When the boys came to Birmingham the theatre was just by all the bus stops, so we made a great big banner with 'WE LOVE FLINTLOCK' on, and hung it up on the 37 bus stop, I think everyone in Birmingham saw it".
…as told by Grace Hargreaves (who else!!!)

"It's so good to relive these moments again. Memories just come flooding back. Wish I could find my diary, but sadly I think it got lost during a house move. These were such happy times".
…as told by Carole Garrett

Not only did we get the 'rush' from the concert and the meet's with the boys, my life for one was one long 'rush'. It began rushing to get home from school to see them on the television. Rushing downstairs to get to the phone in case it was one of the 'flinty-girls' calling. Rushing to the phone box at the top of the road. Rushing for buses and trains. Rushing to concert halls once you'd got off said buses and trains. And then rushing out of concert halls to stage doors after concerts! Then at the end of each event rushing to get home or to a B&B. So I've quite possibly answered my own question. We lived off excitement and adrenaline.

The 1977 tour gave us so much enjoyment. It also gave me a little stress!!! Much as we tried, catching the trains you'd planned to get, didn't 'always' happen. Sometimes that was at the fault of the show, for whatever reason, slightly running over, or the total excitement of the 'stage door antics' making you forget how to use a watch! Or the odd occasion when the train's just didn't run on time! Shocker, can you believe that? This in turn would mean you missed other train/bus links. Due to this, there were, and not many I should add, times when I/we would arrive home at 'Silly O'Clock'...this was a time when we would be at least an hour later than the time promised, arranged, agreed. One particular night returning from a concert in Birmingham, we (Viv and myself) had missed our planned last bus, which meant we had to get two other buses, consisting of a huge detour seriously adding on time. We eventually rolled up at my house at just before 1am. My poor Mum was beside herself and as we walked in she showed all the signs of being annoyed and relieved. The following day my Dad (who worked nights at the time) gave me the lecture of all flippin' lectures, he was not happy "Didn't you think to phone? Ya Mother was worried sick, don't ever do that to her again, in future when you get off the train get a taxi". I understood perfectly that I was in the wrong, but stupidly tried to take the emphasis from 'me' by saying "Well, Lou hitch hiked on the A1 to get to a concert last week"..............it didn't work....Of course it didn't. He just glared at me and said "I hope your listening. I take it you still want to go to these shows, what have I just said uh?".........and he stood waiting for me to repeat the

lecture.........Well, there was no possible way I was going to miss out on any concerts so........... "In future when I get off the train I must get a taxi...... I promise" I said.
And with that, normal service was resumed.

Chapter Seven... Carry Me - By Taxi - A Little Of The Way!

The date was 24th September 1977..........the destination was Wimbledon......The Wimbledon Theatre to be exact. The first two lines in my diary for this date read.

"Well I will never forget this day as long as I live, it was absolutely GREAT, I'm so lucky to have Flintlock and my friends in my life"

It was an early start, we had to leave my house at 6am, and I say 'we' as Linda had stayed at mine the night previous and Jane and Sue met us at the bus stop to get the 6.15am bus. Friends Jane and Sue had never seen the boys in concert before, and while Linda and I were 'old hands' at this sort of thing by now there was a giddy vibe coming from the girls that we also enjoyed. We got to Nottingham station, and as we had time to spare before boarding our train we had some photos done in the photo booth. At 75p we couldn't waste a penny so we all scuttled in and out as fast as possible to catch the flash going off!! Go!!!! Me and Linda - Me and Jane - Jane and Sue - Sue and Linda. Eventually the strip of photos fell into the tray and I proceeded to waft them dry as we went down the steps to get onto our platform. Our 7.15am train arrived and before long, we were off. Bev joined us, popping on the train at Leicester. On reaching London we met up with Tina, Julia and her sister Carol. We were all talking for England on the way to Wimbledon, even passing around the 'Wrigleys' didn't shut us up, already very over excited and it wasn't even midday! Finally got off the train and walked down the high street to the theatre, it was 11.35am when we arrived and there were already 20-30 fans outside. Jane and Sue were really excited by now, and Linda said "oh, you two hee hee we've got the whole day to go yet, ya better calm down". We stood around chatting and getting up to date on the gossip. Some of the fans had recently purchased new badges from the fan club, and were proudly showing them off, there was lots of envious 'oowwing' and 'arrring' going on. It was just before 1.30pm when Newton arrived and most of the girls, Jane and Sue included thought it was the boys arriving, so ultimately ran after him! Approximately 20 minutes after that as I sat on the steps to the main doors of the theatre I heard this girl 'scccreeeeeaaam', and looked up to notice 'Flinty' moving towards the theatre being driven by Big Mick with 5 lovely people inside. (I'm talking about Flintlock, not the Jackson Five…..although I'm not knocking them, hey they produced some great music). I was up and quick as a flash at the stage door. As it stopped just in front of the gates/stage door of the theatre I saw the now infamous Grace jump onto the roof of the car and in an instant the fans had covered it, everyone was screaming and banging on the car! I remember seeing Derek put his hands over his ears. It must've sounded like thunder to the boys inside. I was right at the side of the stage door entrance. I'd had my fill of being a car sandwich so opted for the slightly safer option. Sue was right at the side of me, and as Big Mick got out of the car she kinda flung herself half in and grabbed hold of Mike. At the time it surprised me to be honest as I never imagined she'd be quite so 'full on'. Big Mick tried to pull her away from him, and then a bouncer appeared from inside the theatre and had a go at pulling her away too. She was screaming "Miiiikkkeeee"………. ouch! She just wouldn't let go, there seemed to be utter chaos during this, the screams were deafening and fans were going crazy, you couldn't see the car as it had been smothered by so many girls, and still, Sue didn't let go. Big Mick tried, the bouncer tried, Mike tried. Nothing worked. This girl could grip, fact. I can see Mike's face now, his usual cool and controlled approach had been scuppered by Sue and he looked rather worried. I didn't blame him though this was organized chaos on a serious scale. I noticed Sue seemed to be going ever so slightly hysterical, not in a good way, it began to feel very wrong so I got hold of her arm, pulled and shouted "Sue, stop it, just let go nowwww", and oddly enough, she did! Be it with dramatic hysteria, a rag doll flop and many tears. Big Mick nodded towards me and mouthed 'thanks love', and with that the bouncers made a kind of tunnel for the boys to get out of the car and into through the stage door. We were jostled about a while until all of the boys had got in, what should have taken less than 30 seconds took about 15 minutes. After they were in we decided to walk around to the front entrance where Jane but mainly Sue spent the next half an hour crying. First concert ya see, gets 'em every time.

During the afternoon our Wimbledon girls, Lynne, Lorraine, Gill, Lisa, Terry and Julie arrived and much fun and jollity followed, from trotting up and down the high street on the hunt for chocolate, to singing Flintlock related songs whilst sitting on the steps of the theatre…….eating chocolate. While all this was happening we also purchased, our by now compulsory, carnations and roses…..and met up with other fans, Jenny, Jackie, Lauren and Dawn to name a few. Jane and Sue were enjoying the process of the whole day, and kept going in and out of the singing, crying, singing, crying mode. There were a few girls who had brought with them small photo albums so they too were doing the rounds. We stood at the gates of the stage door entrance listening to the boy's sound check…..1, 2 test, 1, 2, 1, 2, test…… you could hear this from inside….and 'that' made Sue cry again! I think at this point Linda was digging a tunnel underneath the theatre to gain access, she was like that was little Linda.

Whenever we got to a theatre one of the first things we'd do is investigate around to suss out possible access means. Me? Well, I like to think of myself, then and now as reasonably sensible, (hands up – who laughed then?) so why did I end up within seconds during the sound check, trying to climb over a fence a little further down from the theatre? Well, I did climb over a fence there was no trying in it. I was immediately 'lifted' by a gentleman from muscle monthly! And his "oh no ya don't"....was responded with "oh yes I do" line. I couldn't help myself, I've always loved Panto. His effortless lift had me landing quite promptly close by the main door area, which was swiftly followed by some of the girls being escorted out of the building via the main entrance to a rousing cheer from the fans! Nice one Fran. Heck that security was good.

The first time I recall meeting Fran actually was climbing over a fence! But that was such a normal instance of who we were back then.

"As we always arrived really, really early for gigs, we noticed a tiny window open by the circle hallway. I think four of us climbed up the drainpipe - must have been a really easy climb to put our feet on - we found our way into the back of the circle seating area. The boys were doing a sound check. So we sneaked down to the front of the circle where we got caught, boo. As they threw us out by the front entrance we all got a huge cheer from the other fans waiting outside. To this day I can't believe we did this".
...as told by Fran Norton

At 5.30pm, unusually early, we were allowed into the theatre, but there was good reason, this show was being filmed. This concert stands out for me so much because on getting inside I have never spoken to so many other fans, some that I knew, and others I didn't. It was such a friendly atmosphere. A line in my diary for this date quotes.

"You meet some really lovely people at FLINTLOCK concerts, I feel like I've known these girls all my life".

And it was a fact, you did. I was dressed accordingly for such an occasion. 'Flintlock tee-shirt', silver metal 'Flintlock' 'f' necklace, jeans, black bomber jacket with sequinned 'F' sewn on the back, and a felt black hat! Covered in sequins with the boys names on and love hearts, and assortment of badges and rosettes, oh and my trusty scarf. Yes, I'd gone all out to promote 'my band', there was no doubt to Joe public who I supported. My black and white trim bomber jacket had been recently purchased from 'Chelsea Girl' for £4.99, how we loved that shop, and over several nights previously I'd lovingly sewn a silver sequined Flintlock 'F' on the back and some hearts on the sleeves. Some of the girls had made banners, and while these were great you always hoped you wouldn't be sitting behind anyone with one. This, like all the concerts was a sell-out…..and so we felt lucky in that we'd managed to get tickets at all, we were just a few rows back, slightly off centre.

The stage was vaguely lit, and then as the lights went up Newton walked out onto the stage………..and the screams began. Jane turned to me and said "Shelley, owwwwwww, I can't believe this" in a half scream, half appreciation of the event kinda fashion. Eventually with a l o t of persuasion Newton got the screams down to a respectable level while he explained to us, this concert was being filmed for Japan, Canada, Australia, Switzerland and various other countries……………..but perhaps not the U.K.! As in the history of it being made, I've never seen it, and neither have the girls. Newton looked very dapper and obviously had made that extra bit of effort due to the cameras. He explained that the auditorium was lit as we were also being filmed, and asked us to sing along, have fun, and smile if we noticed a camera on us, that's an awful lot to remember when you just want to scream for the band to notice you!

The boys walked out onto the stage in new outfits, very silky and in some cases sparkly! The music began and the camera's rolled. I asked the girl behind me to take a photo of the stage in-between my head and my scarf held in the air, which she kindly did, and I still have. By the end of the show my arms ached so much from all the waving of my hands, my scarf, my hat. We did as instructed and enjoyed the concert with every bit of enthusiasm we had. A few fans rushed the stage….here we go, rushing again!.....Linda and Sue went down to the very front of the stage, but Jane and I stood on the steps of the third row so that we were level with the height of the stage, and no sooner had we got there Mike and then Derek acknowledged us. Jane burst into 'happy tears' and a 'John fan' at the side of me gave me an impromptu hug and said "I'm so happy for you"! (You know that 'thing' that people do when they've had a few drinks, and insist on telling everyone how much they love you?……..Well, it was like that, without the alcohol.) As I said previously, very friendly fans these. 'Learn To Cry' made the vast majority of the audience live up to its title….during this I noticed a camera zooming in towards me and so whilst swaying I tried to look 'thoughtfully reflective'. It quite possibly came out as, 'Did I remember to phone me Mum after I put my train ticket away – by Confused of Nottingham?' Towards the end of the show, Newton was back on the stage………determined to get in the film! Ha ha……….and said "Right let's see, there's a Jamie fan up there", and with some gentle persuasion, and egged on by the surrounding fans got the girl to wave her scarf for the cameras, that read 'Wotshername Love's Jamie'……..You did understand that wasn't her actual name yeh!

Here are my diary scribbles.

"………after the girl had held up her JAMIE scarf, Newton then said as he pointed to them, 'oh and there's a BILL fan, oh and DEREK and JOHN fans', and walking across the stage he pointed over to me and said 'and there's a MIKE fan'… it was dead embarrassing as I was when I last saw Newton, but since the beginning of the tour I had my DEREK scarf, so I felt daft and just hid my scarf 'n' went, Wooooooo woo woo………..Jane laughed her head off….He said, well you all look brilliant tonight, arrh wasn't that nice of him…………………I hope he wasn't just creeping".

My 'new' scarf was a bit of an embarrassing moment………Sorry Mike, but I was a young teenage girl, and that's how we rolled. After this, Newton began to announce where some of the fans were from, and each time he said an area the fans went wild. (Bearing in mind the boys were still on stage at this point). He actually started by saying 'The Wimbledon Gang', of course they whooped it up, and we also cheered on their behalf, well, why not they were our pals after all. He then went through a list of London, Sheffield, Manchester, Newcastle etc…….but didn't mention Nottingham. Sue, still down the front, was a bit put out by this and shouted Nottingham 3 or 4 times with no response, then as the screams and cheers went down a little she called out NOTTINGHAMMMMM and some girls from the back of us cheered, and Mike looked over and waved and Derek gave us the 'wink/thumbs up' signal, and all was well with the world again, so little could mean so much, oh yes, it made the night. Before we knew what was happening, the boys were singing the final number and the concert came to a close and it was time to leave. We 'fans' were all hugging one another, it seemed just trying to hang onto that happy feeling a little longer.

"I remember at the Wimbledon concert that it was being filmed for Japanese TV, I pretended to faint right at the front....I got carried over into the pit. They were just starting to sing 'Learn To Cry'...when Mike picked up a red rose (which someone had thrown onto the stage) he got onto his knees and spoke the words to me, looking into my eyes..."they all tried to tell me................etc....And there was me screaming out 'I LOVE YOU MICHAEL', when I was a huge Derek fan!
...as told by Pauline Vincent

In the foyer of the theatre, there was a selection of 'over heated' fans, crying and being cared for by the St. John's Ambulance. Overheated being the apt description here, Jane and I had been waving and dancing about so much, we actually looked like we'd just walked out of a shower. We then left via the main doors chatting to our friends along the way, and then headed for the gates to the stage door area. This part of the evening is so hard to explain. After the concerts there was a 'vibe' in the air, that I struggle to put into words, much as I try, all I can say is you really had to be there. A 'fan' of any band/artiste would 'get it'. The only way it can be described possibly is, for a moment, everything feels perfect, you still have the ringing in your ears from the music, and the hustle and excitement from the crowd that fills the air, you really are 'in that moment' and nothing else exists. Euphoria? For a young teenager with not much to compare it to, quite possibly yes.

There were 'a lot' of fans waiting, and a rhythm of banging on the gates proceeded. I kept my eye on the time, as we had a train to catch from Wimbledon to London and then our train home......we stayed a little longer. I hadn't seen so many fans stay behind after a concert since the New Vic, no one, it seemed, wanted to go home. Fans were inconsolable, screaming, crying continued, as did the banging on the gates……and we weren't even being filmed at this point. I looked at my watch again, getting concerned now as time was creeping by. At this point we'd lost Linda and Sue. There were far too many fans to just 'have a look around' so Jane and I stood at the top of the steps to the main entrance in the hope we could spot them, although we too wanted to stay and see the boys leave, we really had to go if there was any chance to get our train. About 10 minutes later Linda and Sue came around the corner, they had actually been inside hiding, in the hope that once all the fans had gone they could slip backstage, but the security at this concert was red hot so they had no chance. With that we hurried to Wimbledon station and 'just' managed to catch our planned train to London, phew. As we arrived at St. Pancras we'd definitely arrived back in the real world. That awful sinking feeling in our stomachs occurred as we watched 'our' train to Nottingham pulling out of the station. We'd missed our connection by a split second, oh no, what were we to do now? We spoke to a guard who told us, 'that' was the last train to Nottingham the next one was 6.45am! "But" he chirped, there was one in 30 minutes going to Leicester. 'But we live in Nottingham' I thought, he spoke as if it was a 15 minute walk away. On discussion we all decided that being stranded in Leicester was closer to home and better than being stranded in London. We asked the guard if we could still use our tickets and he said yes. As it arrived we jumped on the Leicester train and all the way back tried to decide what to do once we got there. We eventually pulled into the station at 12.45……….'Oh no, my Dad will go spare' I thought……..thinking back to the recent lecture I'd been given. I said to the girls how my Dad had said get a taxi, but I only had enough in the 'secret compartment' of my purse, for a taxi from Nottingham, £4, plus a little change. Linda said she had £3.75, and then Jane and Sue said, "Well, 'praps we could put the rest to the taxi fare". The girls had recently left school and started work, so had some extra money. Pooling our money together we had the grand sum of £27. We then proceeded to walk down the line of taxis outside of the station at Leicester, trying to barter the best deal. It started off at £35, and wavered from £35 down to £30! Oh and that wasn't all......Due to the fact there were 4 of us, we would've needed TWO taxi's, as the drivers were hesitant to take more than 3 in a car, help! Even at the time I felt this was unreasonable, our ages, at that time of night, even 'if' they had been stopped by the police, I doubt very much any action would have been taken under the circumstances. Eventually one of the drivers took pity on us, to the tune of £27, but he did take all 4 of us. As the taxi got closer to home the inside of the car went quieter. Even though I'd phoned my Mum from Wimbledon just after coming out of the concert and I'd said that we would probably be a bit late, (the trick is here, you 'say' that, but when you actually arrive early or on time........extra Brownie points see). Anyhow, I still felt very uneasy, even I hadn't expected it to be this late. It had now gone 2am. The car pulled up outside my house (Linda was staying at mine) Sue and Jane decided to also get out there as it was only a very short walk to their homes from mine. We'd only just got to the gate, when my front door opened and my Dad stood there, "Jane" he called, "come here me duck, ya Mum and Dad are here"...Sue ran across the road to go home, and we watched until we saw her go through her gate. The three of us walked into my house. "So I see you got a taxi then" my Dad said. Then Jane's Mum said "When you didn't come home Jane and it had gone 12 we decided to have a walk here to see if Shelley's Mum knew anything". It was time for me to speak, "Sorry we're so late" and I explained about the train etc....I carried on "Dad you know when you said, get a taxi, well we did, from Leicester"! I thought he was going to choke on his cup of tea. "LEICESTER" he said, there was a pause and then they all started laughing. My Mum chimed in, "Well, you did tell her to get a taxi when she got off the train, and our Shelley does keep promises, so you can't tell her off............." My Dad said, "arrrrhhh, but I meant from Nottingham, not b........y Leicester", but he was smiling as he said it. I went into further detail about our missed train episode, and then we three girls began to talk rather over excited about the concert events. Jane's Dad then asked how much the taxi had cost. When we told them £27, they started off with shock replies of "WHAT" and "HOW MUCH", to, shockingly, even more laughter (Could I just add there, £27, v-e-r-y cheap by today's comparisons....I guess back then in '77 it was expensive!). As it happens, our common sense and honesty was rewarded with the Dad's covering the cost of the taxi, and being congratulated on doing the right thing...............There' a moral there surely.

Here are a few more of the girls' travel related experiences.

"Coming back from Pauline's Quirkes, the train stops at Welling first. Helen gets out and we're saying our goodbyes, and then Helen shuts the door (remember those old doors back then?). Well my thumb was in the crack of the door. OMG, how I didn't pass out with the pain, and I lost that nail after it turned black. Helen has apologised many times since........but I've always said to her, it was worth it hunnie"!
…as told by Pauline Vincent

"I used to get a bus from Stratford straight to Becontree Heath. I think all my pocket money went on bus fares back in the day".
…as told by Fran Norton

"We went to Bedworth, June and me, obviously! We booked into a B&B over a pub for 2 nights. I won't bore with the initial problem but suffice to say the landlady had messed up our booking (probably had too many sherbets). She reluctantly sorted a room out for us for that night. The gig was the next day. We knew we didn't want to go back to the B&B again, but we didn't have enough money to change our train ticket…John's Dad and Big Mick to the rescue. They organized with the roadies that they would take us back to London in the back of the truck with all the boys gear, but only if we helped 'the boys' with loading the gear! It was one of the best hours or so, spent with them, we literally had them to ourselves. June and me were so happy, and I got a big smacker from Mike. One of the best gigs ever".
…as told by Ann French

"Got on a train from New Street to Wigan, and never paid".
…as told by Grace Hargreaves

"My Flintlock trips were fairly uneventful as most of them involved catching buses. Once had a trip to Dagenham which was fine too, it concluded with a lift to the tube station from John's lovely Dad. The only drama of the trip was getting 'to' St. John's Wood, where we spent three uncomfortable nights on Elizabeth's aunts floor. She met us at Marble Arch, the buses were heaving. She jumped on the one that was full up and told us to get on the next one! We had absolutely no idea where the heck we were going. We ended up on the wrong number bus, had to buy an A-Z, and eventually all was well".
…as told by Lynne Brown

"Dorking Halls - 3rd July '76. I went along with Amanda and Lorraine Pratt who I was best friends with back then. Only trouble was, their Dad put us on a curfew that weekend and if we weren't home by 10pm we wouldn't be allowed to go to anymore gigs. Got the train early in the day to Dorking and when the concert started, we heard 3 songs before slowly walking backwards out of the hall, waving and crying at the same time, just so we could get the train back home in time. It was still worth it though".
…as told by Helen Morris

There was an occasion where Mike was doing a PA at the Ideal Home Exhibition in London. Linda and I decided to venture down there to see him, and as I'd never been to an Ideal Home Exhibition before, I was really looking forwards to it. An interesting day……..We arrived, as always, relatively early and looked around various stands, watching demonstrations etc. It was as I expected interesting for many reasons. We met up with a few of our friends and then Mike arrived. He was with Big Mick and Newton. There were quite a lot of Flintlock fans there by this time too. There was a replica of his bedroom! Whether that was actually true or not?…………………… Mike's drum kit was on a riser? He did an impressive little drum solo. (I'm embarrassed to admit not sure why he did, or what it was in aid of, apart from what I'm about to say there is no mention of it in 'the diaries'). I do remember Mike getting onto the riser and as the press, and basically anyone with a camera aimed it at him, he shouted to us girls (we were standing on a balcony overlooking) to 'Move along to the side girls, get in the picture, girls, move to the side, move across, move across, girls move to over to the side", and kept gesturing for us to move along, which we did. We were 'so' loud, singing our heads off. The 'building' seemed to amplify us. If people hadn't have seen us they would've definitely heard us.

"I remember when Mike had his 'bedroom' at the Ideal Home Exhibition. He did a PA and was standing on the roof for photos. We all burst into a chorus of 'Long Time Ago In Dagenham.......' much to the surprise of all the people visiting the show. Big Mick looked like he wanted the floor to open up and swallow him. I went home with Mikes sticks that day. I had so many of them in the end, it got to the point that I think he expected me to ask for them at the end of a gig".
...as told by Ann French

"I remember this day too, we were very loud".
...as told by June Sims

"Yep, I remember that. Mike wore a gorgeous blue satin shirt that matched his eyes".
...as told by Linda Stewart

Afterwards as always Mike was in a pool of fans, and Linda and I got some bits and bobs signed by Mike, managed to get a couple of photos of him, and then were showing Newton some photos we'd taken from past gigs, and various magazine related bits. Linda also (for some odd reason) had been using her train ticket in one of the magazines, probably as a book mark. After a bit more chatter there was a bit of confusion as Mike left with Big

Mick with a large assortment of girls following, and then Newton headed off with a magazine of Linda's he'd asked to read an article in. He ran towards a waiting taxi and hopped in. We were in London, it was chaotic. As Newton's taxi sped off Linda said "Oh no, he's got my train ticket in that magazine"…………Panic! Without a moment's hesitation (and in true 'Cagney and Lacey' style) we too jumped into a taxi and shouted "FOLLOW THAT CAR"…….Honestly, you couldn't make it up. Our taxi driver was on a mission, and I think he broke every rule in the history of driving that day. We sped after Newton's taxi like we were in the 60's classic film, 'The Italian Job', if I hadn't experienced it I would never have believed it. As we were being thrown about in the back of the black cab, we went up on pavements, down one way streets the wrong way, practically around corners on two wheels, through red lights, all to keep up with Newton's cab. It was pant wetting hysterical. In our present day and the huge amount of traffic in London we could've possibly just walked after his taxi now, times really have changed. Newton's taxi eventually stopped outside The Barbican and so obviously, so did ours. "That'll be £5" said our cab driver, Linda threw some money at me and then rushed off to get hold of Newton before he could go into the venue. I gave our driver his £5, and he moaned "Hu! WHAT!!! I could've 'bleep' lost my 'bleep, bleep' licence and that's 'bleep' all you 'bleep' give me". So I just dug deep in my pocket and poured approx £4 extra in change into his hand while he was still 'bleeping' moaning. We couldn't have been driven further than a mile, if that, so even back then, he did alright. We chased Newton up towards the Barbican main entrance shouting "Newton, Newton, NEWTON", he turned around and Linda blurted out what she thought had happened. He looked and said………..No. he didn't have her train ticket, eh?………..but she did……..in her bag. We laughed, we cursed, and then we stood in shock, now realizing we had a good mile or so walk back. But you know something? I wouldn't have swapped that day for anything. It was certainly different, and let's face it how often can you jump into a cab and shout 'follow that car'? Unless you're in a high octane detective series, I'm thinking, not very often.

"Oh I do remember 'follow that car' ha ha, and we ended up at the Barbican! Seemed like a good idea at the time ha ha".
...as told by Linda Stewart

And as my Dad used to say……………"always get a taxi"!

*A gaggle of Flintlock fans —
outside the B.B.C.
... and no — that's not Roy Orbison!
It's little Linda.*

With Newton at Theatre Royal Nottingham.

Cat of the Cheshire variety! ~ with Derek

Radio Station capers. L-R...Jamie, John, Mike and 'Big Mick'. Rediffusion P.A...Mike with Les (shop manager) John, Derek, Bill and 'the card'.

93

In more recent years. Meet up's with John (above) and Mike.

Age 13 in my Flintlock cave — (aka — my bedroom)
Reunion time with some special ladies
Lorraine, Lynne, Gill, Ann, June and moi.

Chapter Eight... Redi, Shelley, Glow.

As Linda and I were regular customers at Rediffusion, it was only natural one of our missions was to gradually wear the manager down so much, he would admit defeat and book 'Flintlock' for a PA. We worked on him for weeks and weeks, until eventually he said "I 'spose it would be nice to get the boys here to do a record signing". Ta-dah!!! So we gave him details of how to get in touch with Newton and it developed from there. This shop had lots of hand painted posters advertising various events etc, done by a local graphic firm. They were very nicely done, but looked like all the other posters around and about the town. Popular company I guess. On a visit a few weeks before the planned Flintlock visit, I just said in passing to the manager "Would it be possible for me to do a little poster for the shop to advertise the boys visit"? He looked at me and said "I don't know? Are you any good"? "Well I have an A level in art, and I'm neat, and if you don't like it I won't mind"? I said. With that he asked me to do an A3 size sample. Within 3 days, I'd designed it, painted it, and got it back to the shop.....He liked..... I was happy......He put in the front door of the shop.....Result. He said although he'd booked the graphic firm to do several posters would I like to do the 6ft banner that was to go over the counter (where the band would be poised to sign the records etc). "Of course" I said, and that same day went to the arts and crafts shop to get the paper, paint etc. It was, as requested, 6ft wide and 2ft depth......(I still work in old money!!!). It took me 10 days to complete as I wanted it 'just so'. I took it back to the shop and the manager seemed genuinely pleased with it. I was happy to just have had a small part in the organization of the day to be honest.

Two weeks later, THE day, October 1st, had arrived. Together with Viv, Jane and Sue we all made our way to Nottingham, a very short journey compared to our previous journeys, and we met Linda at 9am.

The first stop off, or should I say drop off, was Rediffusion as myself and Linda had made a huge card with an old fashioned silver Gramophone on the front, and just to make sure the dentists in Essex were kept busy we also made a large chocolate cake! Not so big I could get inside and go "Surprise", but big enough for 5 strapping young gentlemen to eat. So, picture the scene a couple of nights previous to the Rediffusion event of the year, no, in our heads it really was. Linda came over to my house, and there were the two of us in a cloud of cocoa powder. Mixing and stirring and generally taking over the kitchen. My Mum came in, made a cup of tea and then looking at us both with half a smile whilst glancing over our efforts said "Well, I'll leave you to it then, you know where I am if you want me". So the stirring went into third gear, and we made an executive decision we needed "more cocoa powder". I decided we couldn't have too much of anything, so we threw in the lot, cocoa powder, sugar, chocolate bits, net curtains! Much to our surprise and lots of giggling later, I took the cake out of the oven, and it looked…………well………..like a proper cake!

"From what I remember of the cake prep., I came over to yours Shelley armed with multi-coloured foil wraps from a certain brand of chocs to stick onto the huge card we made. Isn't it funny how I can remember silly little details like that. I had no clue what the recipe was for chocolate cake but you seemed to know what you were doing so I just went along with it and I remember us not being sure if we had put enough cocoa powder in it, so heaped in some more just to be sure hee hee. And you're Mum was a b….y treasure. We shut ourselves in that kitchen to produce our

masterpiece and she left us to it, I remember thinking 'my Mum would never have done that'!
...as told by Linda Stewart

Anyhow after all the effort I didn't want either to get damaged so the manager kindly let me drop them off for safety's sake. As we were about to leave the shop I noticed the nice assistant Steve and friend were pinning up my banner over the counter. I was so chuffed. Just as we were leaving to find a shop for a film for Sue's camera, the manager called "Shelley, looks good doesn't it (pointing to the poster) come here a moment" he said, and took me to one side. "The poster is great" he said "here is a little something for doing it" and gave me £30. I couldn't believe it. Thirty pounds, I mean, THIRTY POUNDS! Do you have any idea how long it would take for me to save £30 back then. I loved making that poster, and there I was, getting paid for it, and very generously too.

We left the shop and made our way towards Broad Marsh Shopping Centre where we found a camera shop. As we walked in I remember hearing the song 'More, More, More – Andrea True Connection'...being played on the radio and we all began to sing along, and do a little dance, well in mine and Viv's case 'the bump'!. "You girls sound happy" said the man serving "We've got good reason to be", said Sue, "our favourite band are in Nottingham today". "Ohhhh" he said "It wouldn't by any chance be Flintlock would it"...A little over excited in full chorus we all screamed "Yeeesss". He carried on "Well, you might see my daughter then, she's been looking forwards to it for the past 3 weeks, ever since she saw a poster in the window of Rediffusion". 'That was my little A3 poster', I thought proudly.

Film in camera, we left the shop and opposite we were the first customers of the day in an accessories shop, I remember Viv purchased a necklace and I got a long handled basket bag for all the 'bits' I suddenly found myself with. We then walked up to Radio Trent, the boy's first port of call. Some other fans were already there, and within minutes of arriving we had trebled in numbers. Many girls of whom we knew. A chap came out and said to me! Why me? No idea "Could you make sure no fans get through this door", "Er, yeh" I said, and he gave me a carrier bag of radio freebies, stickers, pens etc. I dished them out to the waiting fans like a mother hen. About 10 minutes later he was back again. "Would you like us to spill the program into the street"? he asked, "I 'think' so"? I replied, not really knowing what the heck he was going on about! Seconds later we could hear the music of the radio program outside. Arrrhhh, spill into street, now I get it. As if it were yesterday I can hear 'Oh Lori' by the Alessi brothers, and oddly enough in my memory banks and not my reference diaries I seem to recall the Wimbledon girls met the Alessi brothers one Summer day at Capital Radio whilst waiting for 'Flintlock'. I remember this because I really like the song, and it just stuck in my mind. Soon after this it was announced that one of the featured guests on Radio Trent that day would be Flintlock, and we all cheered. Soon after this we heard the dulcet tones of Flintlocks' 'Dawn' wafting around us. Everyone cheered again, and sang along. My distinctive memory about that was so many passers-by smiling. I mean really smiling, as if they were happy for 'our' happiness. It was nice, that's all. An elderly lady was walking by, and the girls on the pavement moved out of the way for her to pass by. She asked "so who are you waiting for"? And we all shouted 'FLINTLOCK'.....she said "oooww, how lovely", and proceeded to have a little dance on the pavement with one of the fans".

As my notebooks remind me it was quite a miss-match show, with a punk band and Pam Ayres in the same program. I guess I must've seen the band arrive, but as I didn't know who I was looking for they could've easily walked right by me. I 'spose I had my Flintlock goggles on and not much else touched the radar. Pam arrived with a gentleman and went into the building passing the time of day with us in a very friendly manner. I remembered thinking 'crickey, she's taller than I imagined'. I met her properly a few years later, and she was a very nice lady.

I can't give a reason, as the notebook memories just say Linda raced off back up to Rediffusion as she'd left something there!? Her brolly? Her purse? Her marbles? Who knows, but she did trot off informing me "I won't be a mo". This girl could've given a Whippet a run for its money. She'd no sooner gone and a white car appeared. It was being followed by a group of around 15 girls. Now unless these people were doing a sponsored car push, we figured it must be the boys arriving, we just didn't recognize the car. Turned out it was them. The white car pulled up as did the black one following it, and the usual rugby scrum followed. Mike got out first, managed to drag himself with girls in tow up the steps to where I was standing and said "Hello there, is this the way in"? I said "Yes", I then opened the door, pushed him in and then as if to say 'no, you can't come in', held my arm across the doorway, and none of the girls attempted to get in oddly enough! What can I say I take my duties very seriously. Next up the steps was Derek...... "Is this the way in? Oh 'ello, they keeping you busy then" he laughed, "Yes, and Yes" I replied, and with that, shoved him through the door as well. John and Jamie casually walked up the steps, signing a few autographs along the way, "What you doing?" John asked, "'Avin my hair cut" I replied, and Jamie started laughing, "Come on, I'm not standing here all day" I said......but you know what, I would have done! Bill was having photos taken with fans, and Sue shouted, "Come on Bill, otherwise Shelley will get stroppy she's got a job to do", and bless him, he ran up the steps and held out his hand for me to smack and said "Sorry Miss", as always the fun-maester and it created lots of laughs with the girls. Newton then followed and said "Hello darling, you are the

nicest doorman I've ever seen", and handed me a stack of round orange stickers, advertising the latest single 'Anything For You', again playing the role of Ma Hen, I saved a few for myself and dished the rest out.
Yes, radio stations were only second in line to concert halls!

"Yes I remember going to see the boys at Radio Nottingham with Carole and Bev. We daren't tell our parents where we were going so Carole and me said we were going to Bev's house for tea and Bev said she was going to mine. I remember on the same show were a punk band called 'The Slits' and Pam Ayres. I was dying to tell my Mum I'd seen Pam Ayres but I couldn't as she didn't know I had sneaked off to Nottingham, but I did tell her years later".
…as told by Alison Grey

"First time I ever met Mike was at Capital Radio. It was very quick but I was hooked".
…as told by Linda Stewart

"I also went to Capital Radio to see them".
…as told by Julyet Harris

"The ONLY time I ever skipped school and that was only for two periods in the afternoon was to meet the boys at Radio Hallam in Sheffield".
…as told by Lynne Brown

We hung around outside the station for quite some time, listened to the best part of the radio interview, got a mention with the boys, and we cheered so loud outside so that they could hear us in the studio. I believe the DJ interviewing them that day, was none other than Dale Winton. In my diary it just say's 'DJ Dale', and it was around this time he worked at the radio station. After a few 'fan' photo's we decided to head back to the shop and so started to walk the five minute journey up the road back to Rediffusion, in time to see the boys arrive. On the way we passed Linda who was trotting back to Radio Trent. It was like doing a relay race!

On reaching Rediffusion the manager was at the main door, he was in a bit of a flap………. "Shelley, could you wait here for the 'group', I have a phone call to make and I might not be here when they arrive to escort them in, thanks dear". Errrrrr, another door! Was there something going on I wasn't aware of? Standing waiting, our friends from all over the country began to turn up, our pals Carole, Ali and Bev from Leicester had walked up with us from the radio station, followed by friends from Hucknall, Sue and Denise. Tina and Julia had also made the journey up from Luton, and our two Guys and Doll's friends from Derby, pulled up in a taxi, yes, Janet and Karen had come along. I had written to them a few weeks before hand to inform them about the Nottingham PA, and they had responded saying they would try and make it. Janet said "look at me" and she had made a large badge with photo of the boys, which was quite a sweet thing to do. We had a little catch up and then Karen said "Ohhhhh looks like they're here", and the cars drove down the road, followed by some…………………..Bay City Roller fans? Yes, that baffled us too at the time………..but apparently they liked Flintlock too (Viv discovered during the afternoon)….and I'm guessing didn't have time to run up a different outfit so just arrived in the tartan short legged trouser attire you'd have expected back then.

The boys were in clear view by now, and there were quite a large group of fans surrounding the shop. Amidst all this screamy-chaos there was quite a comical view, the people queuing for a bus on the opposite side of the road looking quite baffled as to what was going on. The cars got as close to the shop as possible and Bill was the first one out. He reached me and said "I've just seen your twin sister working down the road at the radio station, is this your side line then"? It felt like it! Quite smoothly all the boys were in, be it narrated with screams and cries from the fans, and as instructed I escorted them down the stairs to the basement area. I have to say at this point, it felt really strange. I'd never been in this situation before, and with it being Nottingham to boot………it was just strange. It was as if I'd been given the key to the city or something. Linda had run from the radio station so she was also back at the shop too. She craftily just followed the boys behind the counter, and Viv joked "I don't want your autograph woman"……. Against my better judgment I'd taken my cassette recorder. I wanted to record the atmosphere, (yeh, my Mum looked bewildered too when I said that). The idea was, record the afternoon, or as much as the tape would allow, and then in a low mood of Flintlocklessness (sounds like the sort of song you'd hear in the film 'Mary Poppins') cheer ourselves up back home, by playing it, and experience the whole thing again……You had to be there. Some of us were. We were right at the front, so all the boys noticed it, mainly as it began to be a bit of a hindrance to us, it wasn't something you could just pop into your pocket, quite bulky. So firstly I'd be holding it, then Viv, then me again, then Viv, then……… There was a 5ft high cardboard cut-out of Barbra Streisand, and Bill kept picking 'her' up and dancing around with it, while this was going on I think Viv fancied herself as a reported as she leaned over the counter with mic in hand and said "Bill, when are you coming to Sheffield again"? His reply was "Well, we've gotta go home and get our dinner first"!

On this particular extravaganza, it was the only time we had seen the boys, chat wise, since 'a' Dagenham visit, when Linda and I took 'our' questionnaires for the boys to fill in, so we handed the papers to the two boys who had missed out, Mike and John. Jamie looked over John's shoulder and said "What colour underpants have you got on"? And much fun followed, you can then hear John on the tape say "I'm looking at these questions actually, they look rather, well, rather rather". The manager Les was now in view with a large smile on his face (possibly seeing the 'pound signs') and the shop filled, and filled, and……..You see this little basement area, well, let's just say, if you had 60 people down there, it would have been very full. Fair to say there were easily more than double that amount, and more on the stairs, and more outside, and they 'still' kept coming in……….and breath in……….Thankfully most had come previously showered otherwise it could have been a most unpleasant affair. Every now and again through the chatter-clatter you could hear 'Anything For You', playing in the background, and the cash register, 'tinging' as another sale had been made.' EVERY TIME A BELL RINGS, A FLINTLOCK FAN HEARS THEM SING '…..As the chatter got louder, so did the music, as the music got louder, so did the chants, as the chants got louder….so did the screams! While the boys were busy signing records, books, having photos taken etc, someone had brought in those balloons that once you'd blown them up you let go and they 'travel' while making a loud whining sound, that caused some fun……as did the 'cracks' that were going off……..I have no idea what caused that noise (I'm thinking it may have been caps?). As the first quite loud one went off, I heard Mike say "I wondered what the b………. hell that was", and John said "You wondered what? Wondered what Michael? Watch ya swearing love" (it's all on the recording mi'lord). As if there wasn't enough chaos to be going on with Newton decided to stand on a chair and shouted "Would the girls at the front let the girls at the back get to the boys to get the autographs"……..'Anything For Newton'!!!……..I totally agree now, as I did then. It was only fair that everyone should get an autograph, get to speak to the

boys. However, while Newton saw fit to keep announcing this as if it were on a loop, what he had failed to notice was that, we were packed in like sardines, you couldn't have got a bus ticket in that room...........Yet still he prattled on. Health and Safety would've had a field day. So good thing it happened then and not now as there were approximately three times the amount of people in that room to the number there should have been. A BCR fan behind me........I know, that sounded crazy at the time too, said to me, "He can see that bloke can he? How are we 'sposed to move"? She made a fair point, but I also understood the reason for the announcement. The girls on the stairs now decided to attract attention to themselves as getting an autograph seemed to be fading fast. So their choice of weapon was to sing 'Happy Birthday'. Off they went........... "Happy Birthday to yoooooou, 'Appy Birthday tooo youuuuu, 'HAPPY BIRTHDAY DEAARRR JAMREK'........?...Jamrek? New member? No, a classic example of not deciding to talk to each other about which name you're exactly going to sing first! Jamie and Derek's birthday's being quite close together you see. Nice sentiment though, and soon after the entertaining mega-mix version, they sang the song twice with the appropriate names. The boys waved to them, the girls waved back, then screamed (the girls that is, not the boys!) and a bit more, and a bit.......ouch! I had a notepad in the shape of 'Snoopy' and while asking Viv to "get hold of this" and thrusting the cassette at her, I got the boys to sign pages of the Snoopy shapes, and gradually passed them back through the Flintlock-Rollers-Guys and Dolls style chain gang to the girls on the stairs. Well............I knew how important these things were. During this write-a-thon, Mike asked me if he could borrow my pen as his had decided to blot. Rookie mistake, to this day I never saw that pen again, Mike Holoway you'll be hearing from my lawyer!
The management had put on a small reception/buffet type thing in the back room so after a couple of hours of autographs and

photographs, Flintlock we're invited back there along with Linda and 'moi'. There were still a very large amount of girls hanging around, and each time the door opened all you could hear were shouts and screams of 'MiiiiiiiiKKKKe' 'DEREKkkkk', 'JOHNnnnn' etc.............after about 15 minutes the door opened, and the only name you could hear was 'SHELLEYyyyy'.......Eh? It makes me chuckle even now thinking back. I was sitting with Derek at the time............I know........be still my beating heart. And he said "You're very popular arnt you", it appeared I was, ha ha, as it happened again, and again. I never did find out what the girls wanted, I think it was just 'giddy' kicking in.........possibly for the hundredth time that day. On the way home 'my gang' we're actually saying how they were happy Linda and I had been invited in as we were quite instrumental in getting the boys there in the first place. It was so lovely being in such close company with the boys, good ole Rediffusion. John ate the last ham sandwich and Mike jokingly complained he wanted it so Linda said "Oh Mike, don't be so mardy". A third of the room understood and the rest, well, they didn't. Much fun had as we tried to explain to the southern chaps exactly what 'mardy' meant. If you don't know what it means, you'd better make a journey to Nottingham...............me duck!

"...today was like a dream, Linda, Viv, Jane, Sue 'n' me had the most fantastic day.........everything was perfect, just perfect........in fact better than perfect and I don't even know what that word would be.........."

That was a special time, having a nice chat with the boys. The manager of the shop was beaming, he was talking to Big Mick and Newton saying how Linda and I were two of his best customers, and even after the event, we continued to visit the shop on a regular basis. It was actually a great shop. My elder brother had introduced me to it, and I could see the attraction, you could get your hands on all manner of obscure records. The manager asked me a few months later if I would make two posters for him for an appearance of the pop group 'Child' he'd organized all due to the success of the Flintlock PA, and of course…….I did.

During this little social gathering we gave the boys the over-sized card, which Bill took hold of and the cake which Newton said he would look after. We found out from Bill the next time we saw them that the cake never actually reached Dagenham as they got peckish on the way home. But it served its purpose. It was made for them to eat after all, so all in all quite a successful mission I'd say.

As the day's visit drew to a close I went into my bag and produced some letters that Lynne and Lisa had asked me to pass on to Mike for them. The flashbulbs of the cameras were on over drive, Linda took a photo of me with Derek and then the time came for the boys to leave.

"I remember the photo very well, you looked like the cat that got the cream".
…as told by Linda Stewart

Newton and Big Mick and a couple of the shops employees had managed to get the fans outside, so we all left the back room to walk through an empty shop. It was like a ghost town, and strange to see it so empty after it being so full to the extent you couldn't see the floor. Strange what you remember, but very very quietly there was Amii Stewart's version of 'Knock On Wood' playing in the background, and I 'must've been quietly singing along (I do this and don't realize I am) and Derek said "Arhh next time, we'll come to your record signing"………..gush, and blush. I walked behind Mike and Linda going up the stairs at the side of Derek, at the side of? Who am I kidding, I'd linked my arm

through his, there was an opportunity and I took it. He said "Thanks for inviting us here", "It was our pleasure" I said, as it had been, we'd had such a special day. As we were going up the stairs, Bill who was behind us said "Why do I feel like I'm in a wedding procession"…..I couldn't sleep for a week afterwards with a comment like that floating around my head, ha ha.
Outside there were cameras at the ready, and the manager had hired a professional photographer to do some shots for the local paper. So the horrible bit we always dreaded, where they had to leave us was delayed due to the taking of photos. I stayed close by as the boys walked to the cars, and got hugs from Mike, Derek and John……..Bill and Jamie, were very kindly doing a few more autographs (Girls on the stairs maybe?) and a few photos. Then before we knew it they were in the cars and leaving us, be it slowly due to all the traffic going up the hill towards the Theatre Royal. As we half walked half trotted behind the cars, Linda looked and me and we both said "TRAFFIC LIGHTS", and ran like the clappers up the hill and pressed the 'crossing button'…..'pant pant pant'……These style crossings were relatively new at this time and for us fans, a God send, anything to slow the cars down. 'Just' as the first car reached the lights they changed to red. Around 40 fans had taken chase up the hill and were now once again covering the cars. I grabbed hold of the car door handle at the back on Derek's side, mouthing byeeee and looovvvee yooouuu. Strange how we acted like that when they were ever 'in' a car, when moments before we'd been sitting having a civilized conversation!……. I blame hormones. Anyhow, the lights changed, and gradually so not to cause injury or accident, the cars moved from their standing position rather slowly, picking up speed to driving away, with us fans holding on for dear life. It was only as it disappeared around the corner and finally on its way at a speed we could no longer keep up with, that I realized I was left holding half a silver door handle! Ooops.

Have you ever had one of those moments where you laugh so hard that it actually hurts your stomach and your doubled over, and you can hardly catch your breath for laughing, your crying happy tears, and the more you try and stop, the funnier it becomes and you laugh even more………well, that.

"We had a great day, the boys were so lovely and nice. We were glad they had come to Nottingham, and the fans made them feel very special I think. We did a lot of laughing today. ONE OF THE BEST DAYS. What a fantastic time we had, and then when they went we ran up the hill, pressed the lights and went on red, I was shouting love you and the cars left and I had the car door handle in my hand. Hee hee hee. FLINTLOCK ROOL OK."

Afterwards we went back to the shop saying a few fond farewells to various girlies, and of course the manager of Rediffusion. Myself, Viv, Linda, Jane and Sue then trotted off to a café, with a selection of fabulous flinty friends and chat chat chatted to each other. We also chatted to the lady who served us, and two other ladies on the next table about the day, the absolutely cracking day. There was also much chat about our next concert trip. Who was going where, with whom, and 'meet up' arrangements. It would be an honest statement to say we were on a high.

Viv and I eventually went back home to mine, we really didn't want this day to end, we were absolutely glowing. I think we'd been in the house for the grand total of 30 minutes when we decided…………………….'We should listen to the cassette'. We went upstairs to my room and played out 'our afternoon' all over again, and with that the laughter began again too. For the reasons we laughed in the first place, but also this time around due to Viv's grunting and gasping! Ow matron! We were very squashed in that shop and for the best part people were pushing and shoving, we were trapped up against the counter of the shop. Amongst the boy's chit-chat every now and again you'd hear, "uuuhhhh" and "arrrhhhkkkk", it was funny. When we finally went downstairs my Mum asked "What on earth have you girls been laughing about", and we told her.

The following day Viv was off back home to Sheffield and after I'd walked her to the bus stop it was back home for me too. As I walked into the house I heard the familiar noises of the previous day. I walked into the sitting room and my Mum and Dad were playing the tape and both were in hysterics. "Oh my goodness" said my Mum "Oh dear Viv, the poor girl sounds like she's in labour", and they continued laughing. That tape became quite famous. It was played for every neighbour and relative that visited our house over the next month to six weeks, and brought an equal amount of giggles each time. Everyone came up with the same question "Is she having a baby"?.......Very funny. I recently found it in its original cassette form, and moved it over to mini disc, again to preserve. And they were right, giving it another listen after all this time it really does sound like she's in labour. My Dad insisted I send the car door handle back, spoil sport. My argument of "well, they obviously managed to get out of the car, so do I haaaave tooooo", was just met with "Yes, ya do". So a couple of days later all safely wrapped up I nipped down to the post office on Vernon Road and returned it to the fan club address.......Pity........I might have got a good price on EBay for that now.

A few years after this, I left Nottingham due to work commitments. Yes my dream of singing for my supper was also becoming a reality. On a return visit in the late 1980's I was in Nottingham City centre with my Mum. We were meeting up with Auntie Nora, 'our' Anne and 'our' Pauline for auntie's birthday lunch. Heading for the Flying Horse pub/restaurant, we walked down Angel Row, the site of our Rediffusion shop ………it wasn't there anymore, and I felt such sadness. I just stood there looking at the space where the shop had once stood. That relatively small but precious building held one of my most loveliest of memories. My Mum said how it had closed a good 18 months previously, probably due to a 'Currys' opening on the outskirts of the city. I admit, in broad daylight I actually shed a tear. My Mum got hold of my arm, "Awwww don't be sad because it isn't there anymore duckie" she said "Eh be happy because it was".

Chapter Nine... Bath To The Thames.

Over the 1977 tour, apart from B&B's, there were a few occasions where we girls stayed at each other's homes. I crashed on beds, floors, sofas, anything to save a few pennies. I remember having a selection of fans stay at mine over the Flint-years. One weekend I had several girls staying at my house, and due to lack of beds, and floor space my Mum actually found a flinty-fan complete with cushion and blanket asleep in our bath!, and I bet you thought that kinda thing was just reserved for situation comedies.

This next 'stay' went above and beyond the call of kindness in my opinion.

The Wimbledon Gang of girlies had an old school pal called Anna, who had moved out of the Surrey area with her parents to Bath. Myself, together with other pen pals and the Wimbledon Gang (minus Lorraine) booked to see the boys in concert at Colston Hall, Bristol. We had planned to get a B&B for the night. I seem to recall some of the girls had asked Anna about information for B&Bs for the night, but on hearing this Anna's parents stepped up and insisted we stay for two nights at their home in Bath.......all 8 of us.

I traveled down to London with Viv, and then met up with Karen and the Wimbledon girls at the bus station. We all hopped on a coach and made our way to Bath. On arriving we were met at the station by Anna and her parents. They lived in a stunning three storey stone house, and we girls had been given the huge top floor attic room for our sleep over. The thing that fascinated me was Anna wasn't even a Flintlock fan! This made it all the more kind of her and her parents to accommodate us. We were served with a hearty evening meal and told "if anyone needs to call home, please feel free to use the telephone", how generous were these people.

It was a strange night, all 8 of us in one room. It was the closest I'd ever been to being in the Von Trapp Family. There was 'so much' chat and excitement (as always). I remember clearly as if this had happened yesterday, but due to myself (Nottingham) Viv (Sheffield) and Karen (Pontefract) and the rest of the girls being from Surrey, the subject of accents came up. As this conversation continued I just happened to say how my pillow was really 'comfy'. Julie, said "Oh my God, I love how you say comfy, you make it sound soooo camm-fee" (that was me doing my best southern accent). It sent us all into fits of giggles. Even now, when I say the word comfy, no matter in what context or company that little memory comes to mind. I've always been intrigued with accents so it was a very appropriate subject for me. The night went on as did the chat, now and again someone falling asleep so the rest of us whispering the night away. I fell asleep and then was woken up by the girls as I was having a nightmare. Soon after this the exact same thing happened to Karen, how strange was that. Not much in the way of decent sleep happened, (is it possible to go without sleep for a whole year?).......we we're just thankful of the full tummies and roof over our heads for the two evenings. After the best part of the night being chatted away we decided to get up at 6am. Went downstairs and we were met with Anna's Mum in the kitchen providing us with tea, coffee and breakfast. She wouldn't hear of letting us go out with no food inside us. So after breakfast we left the house and got a bus to Bristol. We arrived at 10am, unfortunately it was 4pm before we got sight of the boys. But we managed to fill our day as usual. Met up with lots of friends and generally filled in the time talking all things Flintlock. In my notepad it says how Gill was quite upset as she discovered a spot on her face and didn't want the boys to see her, awwww. Isn't it strange how things that were of the utmost importance then are so trivial now. Anyhow, like a little army of teenage ants we spread across the town centre in the hope to find a shop that sold 'Witch Hazel' to help our friend in need, and we did. Arrhhh crisis averted.

It reached 4pm and the boys did indeed arrive, as did Newton, Tony Prince and several others. Not too many fans were waiting so it was quite a calm and casual 'get in' of handshakes, hugs, and haircuts??!! John had had his hair cut, and so all cameras were on red alert, ha, Tony was joking how it should make the 10 o'clock news, oddly enough it was important enough to be the subject of conversation with arriving fans that afternoon. The boys seemed happy and relaxed if not a little giddy. Jamie asked us if something was happening there that night, and Bill joked that we were 'probably waiting for Showaddywaddy'…………..as iffy-iffy!

Eventually 7pm arrived and we were allowed to go in to the theatre, and our seats that spanned the greater part of row C were closer to the stage than it sounds. There was no orchestra pit, so row A was directly in front of the stage. There were an awful lot of security guys, more than I'd ever seen at a concert outside London before. It was rather off putting to see 'bouncers' directly in front of the first row, talk about "getting to know you". They stooped as low as they could in order for us to see the show, but never the less….. Some fans behind us who were from Bristol were telling us how Colston Hall was doing a month of 'pop groups', they had previously had 'Rosetta Stone', 'Child', 'Racey', there to name a few.

The show began and I had never been part of such a reserved audience before, the place was sold out but it was all very polite, with appreciative applause, with what can only be described as gentle screams and whoops. Bit of a surprise to be honest. Even the support group, who were quite cute, called 'Stamps' were greeted like we were all out for afternoon tea. After the interval a familiar face walked out onto the stage in the form of Mr. Prince, we all went into chant mode, and the crowd decided to liven up a bit. Tony began to whip up the audience, delivered the big build up and then Flintlock walked out onto the stage and it was like someone had flicked a switch as the fans went into hysteria. We sang along to everything. At one point the boys just stopped the music and 'we' the audience just took over the song. What a sound, just fabulous, a tingling atmosphere that made the hairs on the back of your neck rise. I've often thought how would that have sounded from the perspective of the band. Very special I'm sure. And yes, yet again, I was day dreaming of 'one day' I'd love to be up on that stage, any stage!

We all waved our scarves in the air over our heads and Jamie moved to our side of the stage as if to read them, and then saw that Terry and Karen's scarves had his name on and he smiled and winked at them, to say the girls were thrilled is an understatement. During Rocky Mountain Way all 9 of us (we'd treated Anna to a ticket..........yes, dragged her to the gig kicking and screaming) began to do a little dance routine, the object of the exercise being it got us noticed, it worked, Derek began to imitate the same movements back to us.

"...during Rocky Mountain Way our group did the same dance and it was great when Derek did the same dance back. We noticed just then Mike's sisters were up in the circle watching us. The whole concert was great and even writing this I feel like I want to burst into tears 'cos we had such a good time".

The very introvert Grace from Biirrrmmmm........yes. Was up on the stage like an Olympic runner during 'Learn To Cry'. Much to Johns surprise she grabbed hold of his arm, it was quite comical as he looked out into the audience frowned and mouthed "WHAT"? Even Grace looked a bit confused as if to say "why am I doing this"? She half let go and then got hold of Derek, then got poor confused John in her clutches again. All this happening while a bouncer was heading towards her, John and Derek finally pulled away from her and the bouncer lifted her off the stage. A random fan raced up onto the stage and 'just' before she could get to Mike she was lifted up into the air by security and boy could she kick and scream

'Carry Me' started up and so did the tears. At this point everything seemed to be going as you'd expect………the boys delivered, the fans were crying, the dry ice was billowing over the stage, then all of a sudden towards the middle of the song, the stage was charged by a rather large group of girls who seemed to fly from the back of the auditorium. Several of them leaped up onto the stage which sent the bouncers into a chaotic dash, and one girl in particular who'd just got up onto the stage was approached by Newton coming on the stage via the wings, and a bouncer from the opposite direction. This girl went absolutely crazy, and I mean full on crazy. She was kicking, wriggling, screaming, biting, the bouncer dragged her off the stage and she was struggling quite ferociously out of his grip that she caused him to lose his balance, this was happening at the end of our row right where our group were sitting, he lost his balance and fell directly onto Terry, which had the domino effect. Terry inadvertently knocked Karen over, who fell into Gill causing her to bang her head. As this confusing mad episode continued I felt myself falling and before I knew what was happening, Lisa, Lynne, myself and Viv had also got caught up in the backfire, and we were strewn all over the floor. The show seemed to come to an abrupt end. I don't know if it actually did, I don't think so, but that's just my memory of it. All I recall then were girls all around us crying for various reasons, screams, and security shouting in the distance, "come on, everyone out". We were suddenly surrounded by first-aiders helping us. I was helped up to my feet and taken to a seat the opposite side of the auditorium. Soon after Viv was also sitting at the side of me.

"Hell fire Shelley" she said "what just happened, everything suddenly went bonkers". We'd both, fortunately, only suffered some scratches and bruising. The theatre by now, apart from ourselves was practically empty. Some fans were hanging around the stage, and a few hanging around us concerned.

While the security were rather abrupt with us, the St. John's Ambulance people were very nice. Terry was in a bit of a state, I think looking back she may have been suffering from slight shock, which would make perfect sense. She was in pain with her wrist so one of the first-aid guys strapped it up for her. Umm it wasn't the best way to end a concert, but we had no choice in the matter it was out of our control. It did take the mood down a notch to be honest. Getting outside there were hardly any fans waiting for the boys even though 'Flinty' was still parked up. The few fans that were there were telling us how a nasty chap who belonged to the theatre was telling them all to clear off, so that might explain why fans were few and far between. These fans were saying how our row of seats wasn't fixed securely and that's why possibly how we all ended up on the floor, apparently a few nights before, there had been another band in and their fans caused a slight riot. Without going in again and checking we had no way of knowing if this was true or not. After all people do like gossip don't they and besides things were different back then, the 'no blame, no claim' culture didn't exist. If you fell over, you didn't blame someone for having sneezed in your direction, you got back up and just got on with it.

It was quite chilly so we decided not to wait at the stage door and just get the bus back to Anna's. Already a little subdued, you can imagine how we felt on reaching the bus station to be told by the bus driver, "any chance you can get a train girls, this bus is packed with football fans and we don't want any trouble"………Eh?……….Unbelievable. Did we look like we would cause trouble? Obviously our sequins and satin scarves were quite threatening towards hardened footie fans. Terry demanded we were let on the bus (I think she'd had enough at this point) and all the football fans started shouting towards us, banging on the windows and growling "Bay City Rollers are c**p"……….Interesting, our sequins and scarves were not only threatening, they caused word blindness! I said to Viv, "I just want to get back and get a hot drink now", she agreed and within less than two minutes a bus inspector just across the way called "Girls, over here", and there stood an empty bus, it seemed just for us? We weren't bothered, at that point in the evening we'd have shared it with people on their way to Strangeways! It was just such a relief, if not bizarre. As we piled on the bus, 'Flinty' drove by us………….. we just looked at each other and said "nah, too tired, home". Thankfully Helen managed to have a more memorable day for all the right reasons.

"Although every show was fantastic and I met some lovely fans at each and every one, the best one for me was Colston Hall in Bristol on 12th April. It was my 17th Birthday on the 13th and I have the most wonderful memento that I still treasure, a huge birthday card that Ann, June and Lynda had got signed by all the boys, crew, friends and anyone else passing by. Then at the end of the show I was covered in shaving foam! We had a lift back to the hotel where the boys were for a drink - only coke though as we were still under age - Then we huddled in a phone box until our train arrived about 3-4am to go home, a terrific day".
…as told by Helen Morris

By the time we got back to Anna's her family had turned in for the night. Anna's Mum had thoughtfully left us all hot chocolate, it was so welcome, a chocolatey hug if you will. So we took our cups of hot choc up to our room, discussed the evenings happenings and then went to bed……………………………and slept! I know, I'll alert the press.

The following day we all gathered our belongings together and said our goodbyes to our very hospitable hosts. Anna had the Wimbledon girls laughing as she was apparently doing a very canny impression of an old school teacher of theirs called Miss Whale. While this was going on Mrs. Beddis called myself, Viv and Karen into the kitchen and covering the large table were 8 sets of, a packet of crisps, apple, chocolate bar, sandwich and a drink for the journey ahead. I will never ever forget this family's kindness. We were all very grateful.

In all the concerts, personal appearances etc I'd been to it was 'the only one' where Id witnessed any real 'bother' and injury………and that aside, can you believe, we still had a great time.

A couple of days after the Colston Hall gig we all went to Dagenham in the hope of seeing the boys. We made our way to Derek's house first. I don't recall why……in my notepad it just says "didn't want to bother Derek's family"….which may explain why we didn't knock on the door. Yes, yes, I know, it is a long way to then decided 'we won't knock'….but the mind of a teenage girl is a complex and complicated one. So, there we were, we'd been sitting on the grass to the side of the property eating 'Love Hearts', and suddenly noticed Mike had come to the front door which was a surprise. We had a gift for him, we always had gifts for the boys, and we'd taken it in the hope one of the lads would pass it on. Mike said we were too kind and told us to stop buying gifts as we must use all our money. We had a short chat and then photos with him and Viv got some things signed. He went back into the house and then about half an hour later, Derek came out. We were hanging by the back gate and that is where he appeared, he walked over to us and gave us all a hug and asked if we were OK, as he'd heard about the Colston Hall upset at the concert a couple of nights previous. He said as he walked off the stage he could see a huddle of confusion and didn't quite know what had happened. Then the news reached back stage, he said he thought it might have been us from the description. He was very concerned that we were all OK. I remember Jane had asked me to get Derek's autograph if it was possible on a magazine poster, I had it in my bag and said "Oh, Derek, could you sign this please", he said "Shelley yeh" and while I was very happy at the recognition, I said "no actually, it's not for me, can you sign it to Jane". While he was doing this, he asked if I'd been hurt at the concert. I said "just scratches, the odd bruise, I'm fine though" He said "good, I'm glad you didn't get badly hurt", it meant so much, not only to me, but all the girls that the boys cared. For a couple of weeks following this it appeared we were the talk of the fans.

Lorraine was back with the gang at this point, yeeee! She'd traveled to Dagenham with us. There had recently been a souvenir brochure released, and within that there was a picture of Bill with a white plastic cup on his nose, and of course, Lorraine was doing a full on imitation, she was then and still is our lovely 'big bird'.

The day afterwards a few of us decided to go to 'Arkview' dance studios as we'd heard on the flint-grapevine the boys were rehearsing there. Sadly our detective skills had led us up a blind alley that day as they weren't there. So we decided to 'nip over' to Thames, and a wise move it was as we discovered on arrival, yes indeed the boys were there. I don't remember which show they were recording, and my written recollections are mainly about the next near disaster. Thames Television (the clue is in the title) was near Teddington Lock......... We were on the embankment with many other fans, all chatting, singing, and all of a sudden there were girls screaming and crying. Our first instinct was they had caught sight of the boys until the air was filled with panic and we realized two girls had jumped into the water in an attempt (be it a silly one) to get to the boys. They hadn't taken into consideration how hazardous the water could be and had got into difficulties. Two of the Wimbledon Gang dived in and then throwing off our shoes Viv and myself followed on by wading in with an offer of help to drag the girls to safety. Even though I was only in it almost up to my waist it was one of those times when you didn't think about consequences, a gut instinct just kicked in and we plunged in. As for Viv she wasn't even keen on anything linked with water and swimming so top marks to her for just getting stuck in. This has a happy ending thankfully as fortunately the girls were helped out safely to cheers and applause. It was a sunny day and so we dried off relatively fast. Our reward? We got to see the boys of course.

"The boys stood around chatting to us and kinda told us off for jumping in the water, and then praised us for helping the other fans. Mike was talking to us a bit. He looked at me and said 'you're soaking, you'll catch ya death, get dry'. He was telling us about the new album called Tears and Cheers but kept getting the title mixed up, and Viv said 'what is it called? Cheese and Chips did you say'? I thought he said 'Chairs and Cheese'. He said 'I've forgotten me self now'.

Sadly we had to leave 'the smoke' the following day, on arriving home I was emptying my luggage bag, and my Mum said "Oh heck, what's that awful smell", I said "Ermm we were down at Thames yesterday", she said "Really? It smells like you've been paddling in it"...........little did she know. I decided to wait until later that evening to deliver that little bit of news. When the time came she wasn't too happy with that information, and I do realize it was all to do with worry and caring about me. I did keep saying "but I was only in it up to my waist Mum", but in her imagination I was hanging onto the side of the Titanic. As it happened my Dad got told off far more than me the following day. I came downstairs and Mum and Dad were having a cuppa. With my arrival she then told my Dad about the Thames incident. Now I need to say, at this time I'd traveled to London quite a few times and been to many shows and various 'meets' and my Dad had become rather laid back and trustworthy of me. Mum on the other hand was still holding the title of 'Very Concerned Mum'. After telling him the tale, she waited for a response. He didn't make one, just got on with his tea. It was at that point they became a double act. My Mum chirped "Tony, say something, would 'you' have been so stupid to jump into the Thames" and he said "no.....but then again, I can't swim". She got a little louder "That's not what I meant, tell our Shelley never to do anything like that again", he just turned, looked at me and said "Never do anything like that again". Ohhhh again it wasn't the response she wanted, her voice was getting higher, "Don't just mimic me, tell her, tell her…….she could've drowned". "You could've drowned" he said. He then had a little think and said "But she didn't drown, she can swim, n she did help them gells wee 'er mates, so well done our 'Blue', but don't be that stupid again". Talk about mixed messages. I think it's called a back-handed compliment………………… How I miss that double act.

Chapter Ten... The Waiting Game.

In recent years, it's usually a case of getting in the house at 3am, after working, or just thinking about going to bed. In August '77 I got up at 3.30am, yes 3...AM., we were at Linda's house and the object was for us to get to our destination as early as possible. Linda's Dad drove us down to London and then we got a tube from Seven Sisters.......We arrived at Heathrow Airport at 10am.
Were we about to embark on a holiday of a lifetime?............Or maybe waiting for a long lost relative to arrive from a far off land?..............Or could it possibly have been an interview for a new and exciting job opportunity............Well, no actually it was none of those.
Of course we went there because a certain band from Essex we're flying back from Japan, and we wanted to be part of the meet and greet welcome committee. It was an eventful day, yes that's the word, 'eventful'. Firstly, on arriving, we saw other fans we knew, namely Jackie, Jenny and Alison, and they informed us, that the boys flight was slightly delayed. Oh joy. Maybe that 3am start was a bit ambitious. I had previously got a satin red rose for Derek, as my intuition was telling me it may have a long wait to reach him. Around midday Jenny insisted on going to a flower stall and getting Mike a carnation. We did try to persuade her to wait a while as we didn't know for sure the arrival time......but she insisted she 'needed' to get one right there and then. Upon getting said flower, five older teenage boys started to pester us, for just under an hour we resembled the end credits of the 'Benny Hill Show', with us walking around the airport getting faster and faster, trying to shake them off, only to look around and they were right on our tails. We were teenage girls, they were teenage boys, at first it was funny but as time went on they started shouting quite nasty things at us, and even

though by today's standards it was all quite tame, in fact it was extremely tame, however it was still a little un-nerving and the friendly flirting that began was now becoming quite nasty. Eventually this security chap came over and asked if we knew the boys, when we said 'no we didn't', he intervened, and they were never to be seen again……….well, not by us at any rate.

Just when you think, right, that's that sorted. A man walked up to me and waved £60 in front of my face! I was rather innocent back then, but even I knew he didn't want to buy my Flintlock badges! So I firmly said "no, go away, please don't bother me", and of course…………..he kept following me. So, back to the security man, and thankfully at this point the money waving chap did a runner. This was the first 3 hours of our time in Heathrow, not the most relaxing I have to say.

Another four fans joined us soon after this and said they had just found out the Japan flight was delayed, we told them we already knew this, so imagine how thrilled (er hem) we were when we discovered it was a second delay…………..oh heck. These fans were unknown to us, so after some chat we made an executive decision to go grab a coffee and get better acquainted, take out a small mortgage and stock up on some caffeine. To be honest this time was rather nice we had a giggle, good chat and swapped stories about recent events, we were also chatting about the boys being on 'Chegger's Plays Pop'. By the time our coffee cups were empty, morale's were back on a high and other fans had arrived, so surely it wouldn't be long now before we'd be shouting "Welcome Home"………..or maybe, perhaps it would.

Each time the arrival table came up, the Japan flights were delayed, delayed, delayed.

By this time it was 3pm, some of the Wimbledon Gang had shown up and so the arrival of our friends had revived us all a little, oh and 'Fruit Pastilles'………..yes, the arrival of the girls and these small sugar filled sweeties certainly hit the spot, and gave us a much needed energy kick. I don't remember how many people bound for flights we saw leaving and arriving that day, but it was certainly a few hundred…….it was then I was inspired to write the hit film 'Love Actually'…………………….actually it wasn't, as that didn't come out until years later, 2003 to be exact. Written and directed by the super talented Richard Curtis, but it did inspire me to buy another packet of Fruit Pastilles. Yes, I know it's not similar in any way, shape or form, I'm just trying to describe how filling in the time between 4pm and 9pm was so absolutely mind boggling. I counted the buttons on my coat, my blouse, other people's coats, yawn. We chatted the time away, then after we were all talked out – that in itself surely should have hit the news – we sat and watched. We watched people greeting, meeting, crying, laughing, hugging, in fact, for all intense and purposes, we could've been at a Flintlock concert. I did a-l-o-t of people watching that day. I've always liked doing that anyway since I can remember really. I would watch people and try to decide in my mind what they're lives were like. Or I'd make up totally wild and wonderful stories to make an old man just walking along on his own, to secretly have the most amazing life. I'm just a day dreamer (David Cassidy knows a song about that). During the 4pm to 9pm airport marathon, we drank more coffee, ate bananas, and sang……..Well, it worked for 'em in the Blitz….. minus the bananas, they were on ration. It did pass some of the time away. We also lost quite a few of our girls to the last bus, the last train and parent curfews. Before we knew what had happened, the airport was quieter and so was our group, now a very lean 9. One of the girls had enough cheese sandwiches to feed a small army so we helped lighten the load in her bag. Her Mother had worried she wouldn't be able to afford anything to eat, she was right to, even back then the sandwiches were so expensive.

By now we were all flagging a little, but wait, we saw something on the horizon....in the coffee shop area, two familiar faces from Pinnacle Records. Yahoo!! it can't be long now we thought.
Actually, it was. Yet again the Japan flight still hadn't landed. It was delayed so many time's we heard Ladbrokes were taking bets on whether it was actually going to arrive on that day at all......but I jest. The Pinnacle people came over and had a nice chat with us, asked us where we were staying that kind of thing. Linda and I said "well here, we've missed our last everything, so this is our home for the night". The other girls were the same, we all felt we'd come this far as in time and space, so to give up now would be futile.
The nice Pinnacle people brought us all a coffee, and we were bright, buzzing and just about bouncing off the walls at this point. But it was all good, why? Because the very lovely lady from the check in desk, or check out desk??? Told us the flight bla bla bla from Japan was due in at 11.10pm..........Whoopie-doo, music to our ears. We got this information at 10pm or thereabouts, and strangely enough when you'd expect the next hour to drag, it really didn't.
Soon it was 11pm and we made our way to the arrivals gate. One of the girls during the afternoon of 'The Long Hot Airport of August '77'!!! (Now 'there's my film!) had made a card that said 'FLINTLOCK' on it, and held it up at the gate, ha ha. The flight had landed and people were beginning to come through the gates giving our card waving associate some odd looks. Quite a few times we thought "they're here"............but at that point we had reached 'desperate', and so any male in a storm was Flintlock.

"I went to the airport to see them leave for Japan as well but my train was delayed so I missed them. I was devastated. So I was determined to meet them when they returned no matter what".
...as told by Linda Stewart

There was a very attractive lady who came through the gates with her two children, and so Jackie asked, "excuse me, were Flintlock on your flight", and her reply was "Ohhh so that's who they are". A concept we didn't understand – she didn't know who there were? – how odd. Anyhow, it confirmed for us we were about to see them, and then as if walking through the mist on 'Star's In Their Eyes', there they were, looking fabulous. I held up my silk rose and called in a very Hollywood musical way "Derek". And then Canadian Jenny May held up her wilting carnation and said "Miiiikkkeee" as she half jumped, half fell over the barrier. No harm done though, as we all, including Jenny laughed and helped her up. It was her own fault she'd taken her shoes off.

"We knew Flintlock would be with us soon, and so we kept a watchful eye on things, and they came through the gates. Wow, lovely. I waved my rose and called Derek and he smiled. Linda waved to Mike and then Jenny called him n fell over the barrier, right in front of Mike, we all laughed and she did, we helped her up though Mike told her off for not having her shoes on. I got a hug, from Bill who said thank you for waiting. Derek was yummy and looked so handsome, and I got two hugs."

Along with the boys were Big Mick and Newton. To say they had just had approximately a 12 hour journey, they all looked really rather good to me. I walked up to Derek, gave a gentle hug and said "Hi, what a journey eh, are you Ok" and he said "Oh hi, bit tired, but fine. How long have you been here then." When I told him he looked astounded, "Really"? He said, and so I just said "Yeh". He said "Oh thank you for that, arnt you lovely" and I received a second hug. And at that moment the day's waiting game had all become worth it. Immediately following this I got a hug from Billy boy and he said 'thank you for waiting'. To the side of me I could hear Mike saying "Your mad you, put yer shoes on", referring to our Sandy Shaw tribute act of the evening, Jenny, and of course, Jenny didn't, she couldn't! Her feet were swollen by this point. Linda had already secured a place firmly on the arm of Mike, I walked over to him, said hello and gave him a hug. He was nice and chatty, and then told 'me', to 'tell Jenny to put her shoes on'! Jamie kinda joined in with 'Shoegate', and asked what was going on. So I had a chat to him about shoes and Japan. Quite surreal……too much coffee maybe? Bill had 3 fans fluttering around him so he was rather occupied. I suddenly realized we were John-less, and was told that the poor lad's luggage had gone AWOL. Not nice, and the last thing you want after such a long journey. We had a few pics taken with the boys, some more chat and then without argument we stood back and let them get off home. My my, we were maturing. Did John 'ever' get his missing luggage? I don't have the answer to that one. Mike asked Linda and myself where we were staying and when we said "Well, we're dossing down here tonight"! He said "I don't believe you two, you are great. Travelling all this way for a start and now this, you are smashing". Linda's eye's welled up, and I think it was a combination of the long wait, the joy of seeing the boys, and release of emotions to be honest. It had been a long, and in places strange day. Before the boys left it was hugs all round, I mean, ALL the boys, and even Newton and Big Mick gave out hugs, and then they were gone.

Here we share other 'Japan' type memories….. 'Domoarigato'

"Oh Heathrow, Mike kept sayin' 'put yer shoes on' to Jenny. We waited ages 'cos their flight back from Japan was delayed which meant we all missed the last bus out. I phoned my mother and told her I was staying with Shelley at Lynne's. We all dosed

down in the airport lounge 'til the first bus in the morning at 6.20am! Fans of bands have it so easy these days with mobile phones, computers and the like".
...as told by Linda Stewart

"I entered a competition to spend a week in Japan with Flintlock. I didn't win, much to my disappointment. I was lucky enough to win a cassette recorder. This particular trip they took to Japan I have to say, I almost got on the flight with them! I was with a friend and we ended up with a good telling off at the police station - oops - oh what fun we used to have".
...as told by Helen Morris

After the boys had left we girls then found a quiet corner in the airport lounge and settled ourselves down over multiple seats with our jackets etc as covers, Linda proceeded to take her shoes off, it was becoming the 'thing' to do apparently! All 9 of us were happy girlies, we'd achieved what we set out to do, welcome the boy's home, job done. I think I'd had half an hours sleep, and being a light sleeper anyhow, every sound was in the background of my 'sleep time'. Linda then half whispered opposite, "Shelley are you awake" and I said "Yeh", so we sat up, and before long all of us were on the floor in a circle chatting. We were discussing the death of 'Elvis Presley'. As it had been such a shock hitting the news at that time, so we sat talking about his films and singing snippets of some of his songs.
That particular night, I was at Lynne's, well, obviously I wasn't but I was as far as my Mum was concerned, because 'that' was where I'd phoned and told her I was going to be at 9.30pm. Hence there was no reason to 'phone in' later on........so I gave her

the 3 ring code instead, Ohhhh liar liar, pants on fire! These 'porkie pies' were never to be deceitful in an underhand way, I just didn't want Mum to worry, it was as simple and innocent as that. I agree now that the world can be a dangerous place, and I know all her worries and concerns were valid, but our 'fan lives' were constantly viewed by us through rose tinted glasses. Linda also did the compulsory phone call to her Mum too, and said we were at Lynne's..........it was only a half lie....'ish. I mean, we were in London, and we were with friends. None of them were called Lynne though, oh and we didn't have a bed for the night, minor details.

We sat singing 'Wooden Heart', and other Elv related tunes........a very different repertoire for us, when these three young men who were sitting a few seats away from us called over "very nice", and then called out a couple of requests! The girls began chatting to them, and they seemed OK really not a threat of any kind. Plus there were 9 of us and 3 of them, safety in numbers and all that. Of course they asked us why were we there at that time of night. We explained, and they said "Oh we know of them" and then one of them said, "Isn't the drummer in The Tomorrow People". So they did actually know who we were talking about. We were chatting and about 10 minutes into the conversation one of them asked what it was like to be in the company of a super star! I did think I half recognize one of them but couldn't put a name to him. The 'friend' said "have you clicked who it is yet"? And then said to his blonde haired friend, "Do the thing"! And the blonde haired fella, half embarrassed, reluctantly cupped his hands and said "Please sir, can I have some more".....Eh? So this was the little boy from the musical film 'Oliver'!!! Mark Lester!!! If it wasn't he was certainly an absolute spitting image of him, obviously a grown up version. The thing is, he wasn't bragging, if anything he was playing it down, so to this day I believe we met him. If not then the guy should be going out as a looky-likey act.

They had a flight around 4am, and so we all just sat and chatted the time away, they were nice enough company. Around 5am I got my second wind of energy and I was wide awake, but I'd always been a night owl, so I knew I had the stamina to do an 'all-nighter'.

We'd seen people finish a shift go home, and then come back the following day to start their next shift, it had certainly been an experience. Just after 6am it was our cue to leave the airport, we got the first bus into the city. Arriving there, we said our goodbyes with the girls and went our separate ways. Linda and I then caught the first train of the day to Nottingham. That really was 'a first' as we were usually getting the last one of the day. Once on the train Linda resembled a nodding dog. I remembered my Uncle Reg had one in the back of his car when I was a little girl, sorry Linda. We were both so tired, but I didn't want us to go past our stop, this had happened on a previous occasion so I stayed awake and woke Linda as we were approaching Nottingham. Eventually (and before midday) we rolled up at Linda's house. I called my Mum and had a little chat. She was none the wiser about my airport adventure, just pleased it seemed, A, I had called her and B, we'd seen the boys the day before. I don't remember much about the next four hours or so, Linda and I just crashed on the beds and we were out for the count.

In my mid 20's I was visiting home after doing a Summer Season and having a 'Girls Night In' with my Mum. You know the thing, cake, chocolate and bottle of plonk. We were chatting about pen-pals and my Flintlock days………You see at the highest point I had 72 pen-friends. (And no, that isn't a typing error). So there was a lot to talk about. They weren't all Flinty-fans, but I would say around 40 of them were. I'd got them via the fan club, friends, magazines, and carrier pigeons! I enjoyed and still do like writing letters, so it was a good relaxing outlet for me back then. And in my opinion, there is nothing nicer than writing, or indeed receiving a hand written letter. I'm a dinosaur I know, but I can't see me changing my ways now.

Ow little flashback memory just occurred. When we 'Flinties' would write to each other the envelope's would be decorated with various statements of 'Flintlock Rool Ok' and 'I Love…..' etc….but another was 'Are you a cute postie? If so sign here', and every so often you would receive your letter's with a postman's signature on it! I think the most I got on one letter was seven. Umm apparently we had cute post men back in the 70's in Nottingham, and modest ones too!

So Mum was saying how she loved getting my letters when I was working away. Then we got to chatting about the boys, and 'did I know what they were up to'. So I told her as much as I knew myself at that time. There was no internet so it was all 'what I'd heard via the girls I was still in touch with at that time'. She said "When was the last time you played a Flintlock record", and I sat and had a think and said "I can't remember Mum, but I still like the music". She then suggested I put one of the LP's on. Which I did, she wasn't going to get an argument from me regarding that. Into the conversation, with the boys in the background she said "Do you remember that time you stayed over at Heathrow Airport", and I began to answer her, and then for the first time in a long time I blushed the colour of a beetroot. "Oh, how do, how did you………"

She looked at me smiling and shaking her head and said "I'm ya Mum, I know everything. We have a sixth sense you know".

It appeared on the night I called her from the airport, I hadn't taken into consideration the noises in the background. She just put two and two together and guessed Linda and I were 'camping out'. She said to me, "a little later when I got the three rings, I said to your Dad 'They're staying at that airport ya know'". I said to her "Well if you've known all this time, why haven't you ever said anything to me"? She said "I was waiting for you to tell me one night when you'd had a few drinks, (charming!) I waited and waited, but it's never happened"...............then she started laughing, shaking her head and wagging her finger at me. I said "Sorry, no really, sorry Mum, sorry..........sorry" She said, "I know you are, I never doubted you wouldn't be. At the time, yes I was worried, but you'd been up and down to London quite a lot at this point as well as other places around the country, much as I wanted to I couldn't wrap you up in cotton wool for the rest of your life. When I got the three rings just after 10pm that night, I thought 'Oww that little monkey', but I just had to trust you, I also knew you were with other girls and not on your own. I didn't get any sleep mind you until you phoned me the following day and I knew you were back in Nottingham at Linda's".

I was in shock. I couldn't believe she'd known all this time, and not said a single word to me. I ended up telling her that night all about that Heathrow epic. She said "Oh heck, I'm pleased I didn't know at the time, I wouldn't have let you go down to London ever again or even to Dagenham a few days after". I said, "You can remember I did that"? She said, "You'd be surprised what I can remember about those days, most people I knew were complaining about their kids being sulky, stubborn teenagers, getting into all sorts of bother and at home I had this teenage daughter who was constantly planning to see this group, you were always laughing on the phone or planning things with your friends, and you always seemed to have so much to look forwards to, so it was ever so rare to see you really miserable, and for that reason alone, I thank those lads". I said to her, "I loved those days Mum I had some of the best times". And she said "I know you did duckie, So......... tell me all about it now, warts 'n' all, I've waited long enough", and I did. Giddy girls? Damned right we were.

Chapter Eleven... Packed Possibilities.

By now, especially during 1977 we were doing so many concerts, trips to Dagenham, PA's of various shapes and sizes......you name it, if we could possibly be there, we would. As well as all this, due to the fact we were getting to know more and more fans, there were a lot more socials and stay-overs happening at each other's homes. This was just a time when a few of us would meet up and play the records, look at the photographs, and talk endlessly about our common interest. My diaries etc, log memories that I had clearly forgotten about, and by saying that, it doesn't mean they were/are of no importance, it just means, wow, we really did cram a lot into this time. You'd need to have a memory like a computer to have every bit of it all easily accessible.
Again....thank goodness I liked writing things down. I'd never realized just how many PA's etc we'd been too, great times. Concert wise it became the most natural thing in the world to be in Liverpool one moment, followed by Sheffield......and then a few days later to turn up at Hatfield......to Welwyn Garden City. I'm stating a fact when I say had it not been for Flintlock never at that point in my life would I have visited these places, be it usually to race to a theatre and praise from within. Never the less it is true, I travelled all over the U.K. in order to see the boys perform in concerts, do record signings, personal appearances, pass by in cars! Stand in doorways! Wave through the windows of a second story building........Yeh, that does sound weird, but that's radio stations for you. We frequented so many 'FAB208 Road Shows' that on one occasion in Lancashire, me and a couple of the girls actually forgot where we were geographic wise, almost missing our train due to being on the wrong platform, yes totally in the wrong direction that we needed to be travelling in.

In a moment of madness once, I tried to work out just how many times I'd been down to Dagenham............Let's just say, it was impossible, and that British Rail could've retired on the income. Alright, maybe that last statement was a bit exaggerated. But I'm sure they could've had an all-expenses paid holiday dedicated to flinty-fans. I know friends Ann and June used to go to Dagenham 2 or 3 times a week, so they must surely take the crown. Pity none of us at the time were being sponsored.

If there was ever a 'Flintlock' birthday and no concert around and about that date, then off we would trot to Dagenham, gifts and cards in hand. This particular year I'd made Derek a 'Snoopy' in white felt, playing a saxophone, which I covered in gold sequins. He liked 'Snoopy' so it seemed rather apt. He also liked Linda Ronstadt and Steely Dan......but they weren't so easy to make, so the 'Snoopy' cuddly seemed to be the better option. It was a nice day, the sun was shining and the journey down was stress-free. There we were along with everyone else that had decided to celebrate with the birthday boy, so yeh, quite a few fans. He came outside to greet us in this tee-shirt that looked like a comic strip, with the words zoom and zap etc on it, looking just lovely as I remember. He was absolutely showered with gifts, and he had a smile for each and every camera pointed at him. Everyone was treated to chat time with him, how kind, and there really was a lovely atmosphere. We arrived around 1pm and Derek seemed to be outside with the fans for the best part of the afternoon. I appreciated that back then, but I appreciate it even more so now. Some of the fans decided to leave after a while and went on their merry way to see the other boys. This thinned out nicely to have some one to one time with Derek, and as always we got him to sign bits while having a chat. Linda told him how my Mum thought he was lovely and that she would like to 'Mother' him, he said "Arrhhh that's lovely, I need Mothering me". I have no idea how, but while chatting to him we got onto

the subject of the tube trains. Linda asked what the man at the tube station had said to myself and Jane regarding tickets. Jane said "Oh he asked if we were big 'un's or little 'un's". Quick as a flash Derek raised his eyebrows and said "Ow big 'un's". It was the only time I'd seen him blush, when I donned my school mistress voice and said "Derek Pascoe, one hundred lines, I shall not be a rude boy". It was so funny, and a great silly little memory. Before we left I asked "Derek, can we have a couple of photos with you" and he said "of course". As I was having my photos taken with him he started quietly singing a Beatles song. Having been weaned on these songs I instantly joined in be it softly with some harmonies, he looked at me and said "Why arnt we goin' out as a double act"..........Why indeed?!
A remark like that could last you a month!.................and it did.

"We were outside Derek's and he came out to us. He looked very lovely. There were a lot of girls, and I was worried we wouldn't be able to talk to him, but we did, it was ever so fantastic. He was cheeky and fun, think I enjoyed his Birthday as much as he did. What a great Dagenham-day. He asked me why aren't we going out as a double act when I was singing along with him..........ohhhh"

I was with Viv in Halifax, a 'Road Show' event……..the boys were there to just do a 'signing' and it was one of the v-e-r-y rare occasions (if not the only one) where I didn't see one fellow-flinty-friend. We knew it was going to be really busy as the weather forecast was sunny. As per we were there relatively early, so we stood and chatted to other fans. After a while Viv said how she was bursting for the loo. She said to me how she really needed to go and find a toilet, so off she went. Time passed and before long half an hour had gone and she still hadn't come back, obviously I was concerned. Not wanting to lose our place at the front I called over to a female steward and asked if she could check on my friend who'd 'gone to the toilets'. It was one of those mobile toilet units I'd seen Viv heading for. The female steward did this, and while doing so the boys arrived and the mayhem began. Still no Viv. The boys started the signing. Still…. no Viv. I got things signed, and the boys finished the signing. Still….no Viv. The boys were ushered away to a VIP area. Still……. No Viv? I couldn't even find the steward now, so off I went in search of my disappearing pal. Now it may have been that, people didn't want to get involved? Or it could have been everyone was far too busy with the excitement elsewhere? Or at an outside chance her calls for help were overpowered by the music/fans. But, when I did eventually find her she was in the end toilet of the cubical block, shouting her head off due to the door being stuck. She had no way of being able to climb over the door, so I dragged a pedal bin to the door. I stood on the bin, leaned over and grabbed hold of her, she clung onto the top of the door frame and over the top she came. It's OK, we'd climbed many fences and gates previous to this (Umm, shut up Shelley!). Before we knew it within minutes she was on the freedom side of the door. Lots of laughing proceeded. Then this woman came in, went into one of the toilets, by 'PULLING' the door open! All this time Viv had been pulling the door from the inside when she should have been pushing. Don't ask me why it never occurred to her to give the door a push? We howled with laughter, I mean howled. If anything she was a bit fed up that she missed the signing, even though I did get her a few things signed in her absence. This was understandable, lots of planning went into these things, and she'd missed the whole event. We went back to the stage area where a few straggler fans were still hanging around and they said that they saw the boys leave. With this information we decided to get off and casually walked to the bus stop and stood there chatting about when we got home whether to have cheese on toast later, or poached egg……………………….You

want cheese on toast now don't you?!..............Anyhow, as we stood there gossiping we realized a car had pulled up at the side of us, and yeeeeee it was our lads. They were asking if we were OK, where we were off too. So a mini chatette followed, and very nicely unexpected it was too, and Bill gave us a fruit polo each (yes, I wrote that down, don't mock, it was important information back then). We then drifted back home in a very happy mood. Little pleasures are sometimes the best memories.
Now it's our Viv's turn to share some of her memories, if she can recall how they came about that is!

"In all honesty I don't remember how I found out about the fan club, must have been through a pop magazine. I did request a pen-pal and remember being worried sick that no one would want to write to me. Gill (Wimbledon Gang) was the first to respond and I couldn't believe that someone who lived so far away (down south) wanted to write to me. It seemed like another country to the likes of me that had only ever traveled as far as Blackpool and Scarborough.
My first concert was Sheffield City Hall and it stands out so much for me as it was just the most magical experience. It was the first time I'd seen Flintlock live, not only had I never seen them before, I'd never been to a concert either, so this was unbelievable to actually see them in person, hear them sing, just mind blowing.
Then things really took off. I traveled down to London to stay with Gill. Traveling on my own for the first time so I was really nervous but totally looking forwards to everything we had planned.

That's when I met the rest of the gang, those girls quickly felt like family, especially with Shelley. We hit it off straight away and very early on it felt like I had another sister. After the concert and other sightings of the guys during that break I really didn't want to go home I'd had such a great time. After that, life was Flintlock full stop. Thinking about those times always brings back happy memories. Due to changes in both mine and Shelley's lives we lost touch around 1980/81. However in August 2016 Shelley found me again via Face Book and it's like we've never been apart".
............Vivien Lee – 2016

I know my Mum has featured rather heavily in all this, she was such a support regarding the whole Flintlock era, but she was not so keen regarding one event. We girls were desperate to know if the boys were staying at the Albany Hotel in Nottingham on one of their 'jaunts' there (Anyone click then? jaunt! No? Then you've never watched 'The Tomorrow People'). Ya know something, I'm saying the Albany Hotel, and that is a vague memory, it may well have been another hotel, in my diary it just reads 'very posh hotel', but back in the day The Albany Hotel, Nottingham was indeed 'posh' ☺. Anyhow, with a lot of groveling and promises of hoovering the house for the next month, I finally got my Mum to phone the hotel reasonably early the morning of their arrival and ask if they were staying there overnight, and had they already arrived.
She did.......but not before announcing "*THIS is the first and last time I do anything like this*". So what happened next? Well she called the hotel, and put on her most posh'est and well spooooken voice, and said how Derek was her nephew! (Rock on Mother) she'd heard the band were in the area and had been led

to believe they were staying at that hotel. She wanted to turn up and surprise him so needed to know if they had arrived yet, and if not what time". The lady on reception was most helpful, confirmed to my Mum that 'yes indeed the boys were booked in there', and their arrival time was approx. midday. She even told my Mum the room number so that she could go straight up to the room when she arrived at the hotel. My Mum was quite giddy, whilst trying to be the sensible parent when she came off the phone........"Now go on, I'm not doing that again". She tutted and then said. "I hope it's worth it, I don't know, you girls". There were four or five of us who ventured to the hotel that day. No badges, no scarves, they were safely packed away in our bags, but there was plenty of make-up to be had and in my case a navy blue velvet jacket and trousers combo. I was rocking that whole 70's girl about town look! The hotel had security on the door, but didn't check details too finely, in fact, not at all! As I managed to just walk past them, with a copy of the TV Times folded under my arm (there was an article in there regarding Mike in The Tomorrow People). Actually this may well have been around the time that the whole band were featured in two episodes of The Tomorrow People, typecast as a group called 'The Fresh Hearts! The story was called The Heart of Sogguth. We have to thank writer Roger Price for his faith in the band as it was he that introduced the boys to the power of television in the first place, well done that man.

Meanwhile walking past security I flashed my 'bus pass' at them and said "Jackie Magazine"........and yes..........they just let me walk past, ha. My Dad used to say "do owt with enough confidence and people will believe ya". All I can clearly remember about that particular moment in the day was feeling shaky and confident, is that even possible? I walked towards the lift, hearing all the chants of the fans outside behind me. The next thing I heard a voice shout, "Wait, hee hee wait, hold hee hee the lift".......it was a voice I knew very well, and there was Linda in her very glam white cat suit smiling like 'ironically' a Cheshire cat heading in my direction. We huddled in the lift and the doors closed. "OHHHhhhhhhhhh hee hee hee hee" on realizing we were alone secured by the lift's four walls. We were practically hyper ventilating with the sheer scale of excitement. Lift doors opened and there we were on the good old 3rd floor, just heading towards room 31. The walk down the plush corridor seemed to take two seconds………..this was mainly due to us being undecided as to what exactly we were going to say once we got to the door. Errr, we hadn't really thought this through any further than getting into the hotel. We reached the door. Linda knocked, we giggled. We could hear some voices and movement from inside and then within seconds Newton opened the door, and stood there with his hands on his hips and said "And what can we do for you two scamps". SCAMPS! I was dressed up to the nines resembling a brunette version of Lindsey DePaul (in my dreams) and he's calling us scamps. Linda giggled and said "Well, hee hee, we were, hee hee, just popping hee hee, by, hee hee, and we, hee hee, thought hee hee, that hee hee hee……………..". I think we may have been rumbled at that point. He didn't seem annoyed with us though, if anything rather amused at our inventiveness on gaining access to the building in the first place. I thought to myself 'think of a valid reason Shelley, think of a valid reason'. So I said "We were just wondering if you needed anything". How lame…… I wish I'd never asked as he then sent us out for burgers for the boys, ha ha. But we did get five minutes afterwards of Mike and Bill time. I think the others must have been hiding. Apparently they had a number of rooms, and this particular one had Mike and Bill in it, and some other gents (I have no idea who they were) looking out of the window at the fans down below in the street in full chorus. I asked Bill what he missed about not being home when they were touring, he said "Me Mum". And taking of

Mums, mine had been given duff information........It's a good thing she didn't really want to surprise her 'nephew' Derek as she was given the wrong room number. I wrote that in my diary and now as I'm writing it again I'm thinking "Should I 'really' be complaining about that"???

"I couldn't believe it I just walked into the hotel, cocky!!!. My stomach was going wappy. I was so scared goin' up in the lift, and we were laughin' our heads off. Newton sent us across the road to the Wimpy for burgers, and when we got back with 'em we had a laugh with Bill and Mike.......no Derek, boo.....the girls wanted to know everything when we got outside again. I'm dead happy".

Our trips to follow the boys were so regular that I had a bag at home which was constantly packed. I'd get home from seeing the boys in some far off town and restock my bag so I was ready for the 'off' at a moment's notice. There was one B&B we stayed in and even to this day, I'm sure this place must have had hidden cameras for some crank TV show. Smile, you're on Candid Camera, no?
When we, Viv and I that is, arrived in the North East, the woman who was on the reception at this particular establishment, and by reception I mean a shelf on the wall of the hallway with a register book and phone on it, hardly spoke to us. It was as if she'd wandered into the wrong house and just decided to 'have a go' at being the owner. She didn't seem to know anything. We asked "Could you tell us what time breakfast is please"? ...."Er, after, er, 7am, no 8am, er I think, um 8.15, praps"........She then half beckoned we follow her up the stairs, so we politely asked, "What time do you lock up, is there a key we could have, we're going to a concert you see and....." She interrupted ...."Er, key, 'er no, no keys, but ring the door bell and 'er someone should be here." (mutter mutter)........It was all a bit vague. We were young,

so we found it amusing and didn't ask much else. She showed us to our room. Oh dear! It has to be the smallest room I've ever stayed in. It was long, quite long actually. But the width of it was the equivalent of stretching out your arms, yes I could touch both sides of the room walls. Maybe we were in a recycled corridor!? The actual beds looked 'home made', and they were attached to the walls so the 2" mattresses slipped off whenever you turned over in the night. The en suite was delightful, a toilet, and a cracked sink. I felt spoilt. The floor of the room sloped, so once inside, you felt as if you were falling towards the window………the very small half frosted glass window that is. There was one small upright chair where the kettle and 2 cups lived, two hooks on the back of the door for coats and a small mirror on the wall. I was laughing at how awful it was while we were unpacking a few bits, and as straight faced as you like Viv said "Are we in prison". Fortunately we were there just to sleep for the night, not hold a dancing competition.

The concert came and went and as always we'd had a wonderful time, we'd seen our lovely lads, we cheered, screamed for England, chatted and did all that was required from a fan. After waving the boys off in their cars, joining in with the chants and calling lovey dovey farewells off we went and when we did finally get back to the B&B it was 20 minutes before anyone came to let us in at the front door. When a house is in complete darkness, yes it does feel awkward to ring the door bell, but eventually a light went on. We could see the first floor had lit up and gradually thru the glass in the front door we saw someone walking down the stairs and towards us. It was a disgruntled man in a thick dressing gown, who insisted quite grumpy "I'm not the 'bleep' butler". While we must've said 'Thank-you' and 'Sorry' several times, he didn't look at us, just shuffled off back up the stairs. We felt bad waking up the owner like that, but we had asked previously about a front door key, and we'd paid for our room, we weren't likely to stand out on the pavement overnight. It wasn't until the following morning we discovered, the chap who let us in was a guest! I embarrassingly thanked him again for letting us in, stating I didn't realize he was a guest, sorry about waking them up etc, and backed by his, I presume wife he seemed a little more approachable. Our night wasn't without drama. There was no hot water, so we had to boil the kettle for washing purposes, as well as drinks. My Mum had lovingly packed all manner of eat-a-bles and drink-a-bles into my bag, and we were grateful. The, er adventure? would've been really hard work had she not have done. There was a communal toilet on our floor (told you we were spoilt) and it was like Piccadilly Station for most of the night, as each time someone used it the pipes bang, bang, banged until the water system calmed down again. Our room – ha, room! – was at the front of the building and there was a night club opposite and so the 'thud thud thud' of the music was continuous until just after 2am. Hard to believe, but we laughed most of the night away, what was the alternative? In the morning just before 8 we went downstairs to see our makeshift 'butler' and partner, a couple of other lost souls, and the owner. She came over to us and asked us "What do you want"…..there wasn't a hint of a good morning or a cheery hello…."Could we have two coffees please" I said, with a hopeful smile………"No" she replied, "Only tea". Viv said "Well could we have two teas then, and full English each please"…….."No"….she growled again "You're too late for full English, you can have toast, or an egg"…….. We sat looking at each other, and she of no fixed personality just stared out of the window. "Why can we not 'ave a cooked breakfast like"? asked Viv. "Because you're late, cooked breakfasts finish at 7.45am"……It all got very confusing. Viv was just about to correct her as 'she'd' told us those breakfast times, when I nudged her under the table, I really didn't have the energy for all this. Anyhow I ordered egg, and Viv ordered the toast……….And that's what we got, delivered to us, by an equally grumpy looking man. I had a very hard boiled egg, and nothing more, and Viv got one slice of bread, toasted. I can hear Viv moaning now. She was having the rant of all rants. My warped teenage sense of humour found it so funny. During those times, I stayed in many B&Bs, a couple of hotels, and most were fine to really quite nice. Yet I can hardly remember them, and in my notebooks, it just reads things like "We had a nice room at bla bla B&B"……..But for the B&B that resembled something out of a Hammer Horror film….I wrote in full detail. It made 'Fawlty Towers' look like 'The Ritz'. I remember it very well, and it has given me some mileage over the years when I've been in the company of people discussing nightmare places they've stayed.

"Our room is ever so small, and we've had to put our bags behind the door, 'cos there was nowhere to put stuff. Viv put her mirror on the floor and it rolled down to the window, we thought it was right funny. The toilet on the landing kept us awake most of the night as lots of people were using it and it kept banging when they flushed it. The nightclub was dead noisy but they were playing K.C. and the Sunshine Band quite a lot so we kept singing along to it. I phoned home and pretended it was OK 'cos I don't want me Mum to be worried about us".

During concert times I only ever got up on the stage once. It wasn't around the early days, more middle ages! We were getting to know the boys at this point. I 'think' this was Hull. It is listed in the month of the B&B from hell! So meanwhile at the concert, the boys were about 5 or 6 songs in and it was a pretty noisy and frantic show regarding the fans. I was down at the front of the stage towards the left hand side. Absolutely jam packed with over-heated, over-excited girls. I have no idea why I decided to do it, apart from the fact lots of fans seemed to be getting up on the stage, and I remember thinking "Should I"? Before I knew what was happening, with the help of a trusty leg up from my pal, I just decided to jump up on the stage. How exciting! 'Hey I was on'. I ran over to Derek, without being stopped. Everything almost went into slow motion. I was really on my way, getting closer and closer to Derek, just passing by behind John and then….there I was, I'd arrived at the side of him, and I just………………….Froze. It felt like one of those nightmares you have where you're in the middle of a shop naked! No? Just me then. So it begged the question 'What the heck was I doing'? It was only two weeks before I'd been standing outside his house chatting to him, you know, like a human. This wasn't the best decision I'd made. While he carried on singing he looked at me a bit surprised and I just gently stroked his arm, smiled and in what can only be described as a set grin said, "Hiiiiii", and then ran back from where I'd come. Not my proudest moment, hence it being a total one off occasion, but I can say I've done it. I just presumed in the frantic dash someone would have dragged me off the stage before I reached my subject matter……………they didn't.

A few weeks later and there we were in Dagenham, and it was one of the few times I remember the weather not being so kind….a bit cold and grey. Linda said to me, "Oh a-up Shelley it's black ova Bill's mothers", and glanced up at the dark grey clouds. Derek was outside chatting with us and confusingly said "but Bill lives over there", of course Linda and I fell about laughing………..and again, I'm thinking you possibly have to live in the midlands to understand!!!

Quite without prompt Viv began to tell Derek about the awful B&B we'd stayed at. Her absolute disgust for the place and I guess her strong Yorkshire accent made it all the funnier, and bless her, she was being serious. So it created a lot of laughter. Derek pointed at me and said "Ahhhhh, righhhht, you got up on stage"......and my feeble attempt at keeping a low profile of that embarrassing episode had been blown. I sort of stammered back, "um yeh, er, but well, um yeh, well yeh". He stood there looking at me and smiled and said "You mad woman". I know! I know!......................I'm blushing at that memory even now. If anyone wants me I'll be at embarrassingmyself.com.

Chapter Twelve... When It Was Taken All Away.

'Here she comes now singing Mony, Mony'! Flintlock released their cover version of this in '78. It was already a 'Tommy James and the Shondells' 60's classic so at one of our house parties having a family 'doo' I craftily put my Flintlock disc on the turn table and loved it when without question everyone of all ages danced and sang along in an unrehearsed but rousing choir.
1978 started off with the same excitement that 1977 had given us all the way through. Gradually however as we got towards the latter part of the year that feeling of total comfort that we'd come to know and love regarding the boys was beginning to waver a little.
THE BEGINNING OF THE END?................This is exactly how I opened up a chapter in my last notebook. I read it for the first time in years the other day, and I mean in y-e-a-r-s. It filled me with the same feeling of upset it did back then.
Yes, this was the year when things began to change.......... Damn you 1978...................well, apart from the introduction of Kate Bush on the music scene, swooping in like a mystical fairy. Her arrival was nothing short of fabulous.
Times they were 'a' changing. Punk had hit the charts with such force, that anything previous was hanging on by its finger tips. No matter what you thought about Punk Rock, you couldn't argue, it was new, very different, and very popular. I admit myself I was partial to a bit of 'The Stranglers' and 'Siouxsie and the Banshees' now and again. Due to our ages, the fans were changing too.
Some were now in jobs, had serious boyfriends, or indeed both. Dare I say, in the world of Flintlock, from September to late '78 it was a very uneasy time. Nothing was as secure and steady as it used to be, everything was a little 'up in the air'.

Mike was now popping up on all manner of TV programs, in fact I remember one Monday evening my Mum sitting down to watch a program called 'Whodunnit', and there was Mike on the panel. The idea was there was a play with a crime (usually a murder) committed in it and then the panel had to work out 'Whodunnit', umm title gave that bit away really didn't it. Well I'd nipped out of the room to answer the phone (why were they always in the hall?) and I recall Mum calling "Oh I think Mike's solved it, the woman at the side of him (actress Anna Dawson) has just said 'well follow that'", obviously referring to Mike's explanation of what he thought had happened". So, Yeh, Mike didn't seem to be as fully dedicated to the band side of things any longer, and was obviously stretching his wings as other opportunities came his way.

Due to some problems with his voice Derek seemed to be doing less and less lead vocal too, so his saxophone talents were doing their bit more often.....and there was a new chap in the frame by the name of Jimmy Edwards. Much as some of the fans tried to dislike him, the 'huddle' of girls I knew and hung with were OK with his arrival. He was alright actually. I didn't do a ticker-tape parade to welcome him you understand, but things were going to change whether we liked it or not so I decided to 'give the changes a chance'. The first time I met Jimmy was before a concert. The chaos and screaming fans prior to a show had eased off slightly by this time, and so to get to the boys to chat was becoming a lot easier, just so long as there were small numbers you understand. So the first time I had an opportunity to speak to Jimmy I did. It was actually backstage.....I'd been allowed in without a chaperone! He was a bit older than the boys and he was a friendly and chatty chap as I remember. I had a photo taken with him, although thinking about it, I wish I hadn't. That comment wasn't in any way a reflection on Jimmy that was in respect of my hideous perm at the time. Anyhow, he was asking where I was from, how long had I followed the band etc. He hadn't been brought in to replace anyone. The band we're now a six piece. Jimmy took over from lead vocal. He had a more aggressive singing style than Derek, and by saying that I don't mean it in a negative way, it just wasn't Derek's sound, his singing manner was far more gentle. The new single 'Hey You, You're like a Magnet' where Jimmy took lead, was great. It gave the band a different sound, I guess giving them that slightly harder edge was maybe an attempt to slightly push alongside with the punk trend. The thing was, most of the Flintlock fans had been a part of the original set up for just over three years, and people, well, they don't like change do they. It was a different 'feel' all round, for some fans too much and so sadly they deserted. I was disappointed as a few were friends of mine from my outer circle. I tried to talk them around, asked them to give all the changes the benefit of the doubt, but they were having none of it. Sad times.....I never to this day saw those girls again.

"The Hucknall girls don't like the new single. I feel strange 'cos I do......I can't agree just 'cos they don't like it, but I don't think they will be seeing the group anymore, which is really sad, 'cos that means, I probably won't see them either. It feels weird. I don't like it. Felt sick all last night after I spoke to Sue".

The concerts did feel different. The fan hysteria that we had experienced and witnessed for a few years had also eased off a little. Don't get me wrong, we didn't sit through the show and say at the end of a song "Oh I say, how terribly spiffing Jeremy" ....but the level of complete hysteria and wild screaming just wasn't there anymore. Some of the concerts were no longer sell outs too. In fact from October onwards of '78 most theatres, while still getting really good numbers for an audience, would be three quarters full, and believe me, even all these years later it

breaks my heart to admit that. I guess nothing lasts forever. We just didn't want to face it.
In the latter part of this year I couldn't go to as many concerts etc as I had previous, I think I must've gone to around a third..........but my life, like everyone else at that time was also changing. I had studies, I'd taken up dance school, joined the Nottingham Arts Theatre and I'd started to sing in the clubs, and also joined forces with a fire-eating act, bizarre! Of which 6 months down the line when doing a showcase with several other acts we set the stage on fire, and I don't mean in the form of thrills, there was actual fire, flames and chaos....but that's a whole other book.
So, yes admitted not exactly the theatre standard I'd dreamed of, but you have to start somewhere, and looking back I was lucky I was able to do this, as it was around that time there 'were' still plenty of clubs to sing in!..........No, no, no, you see you're ahead of me now.....we didn't burn them to the ground.....they were gradually closed due to unemployment etc. You can't have a working man's club if there are no working men to use them.

There was one concert a few of us were waiting outside for the guys to arrive. It was very cold and the boys on arriving like ourselves were in somber mood. As they were walking towards the stage door, there were our usual fond hugs and hello's. Mike stopped, looked at me and said "Where were you yesterday, I thought we'd have seen you at……..'such n' such' a venue". Now this is how much the times really were changing, while I'd jotted most of that day down while travelling home, I didn't even write down the venue Mike was referring to…..shame on me, it was one of those "well I wasn't there, why would I write it down" moments…..
I felt so awful, that he'd noticed I wasn't there, that I didn't go and support them, that I'd deserted them. I spent the best part

of the following half an hour after they had gone into the theatre close to tears. I know deep down Mike didn't mean it like that at all, but woe that was a bad afternoon for me. I honestly felt like I'd let them down. It was the real deal this whole dedication bit.

There were three or four of us sitting in a café and there I was staring into my coffee. A lady that worked there walked by as she was wiping tables and said "You alright girls, boyfriend trouble"? Viv just blurted out, "No, but it might as b…..y well be, this is it ya know, this is is is, it, were going to, to lose them, it's, it's the e'e'e'nd I know it is" and we all looked at her sad little face. I know this may sound odd, but it was a release for all of us. No one in our circle had said those words. We'd just hummed, arrrrd, and shrugged our shoulders whenever that topic had been raised. We didn't want the band to finish, we just didn't want it to happen, and so we had decided, quite sensibly we thought, without saying it out loud, if we didn't talk about it, then obviously, it wouldn't happen would it. Would it?

Yes. Sadly, it would, and it did.

So my last concert was Bedworth Civic Hall, 22nd November 1978. There was just Viv and myself from our 'girls' there that day. Maybe this was the reason, as no sooner had the band arrived we were invited in through the stage door, out of the cold to see the boys. A few years previously if you'd have told me that was going to happen Id have probably wet myself with excitement. This particular day it was like meeting up with your mates. As well as 'us girls' there were a few other fans. I think Ann and June being two of them. We just stood around chatting. It was very pleasant, friendly, calm, but with this underlying feeling of 'the end'. All the time backstage and during the concert I had a lump in my throat, where I just couldn't think about 'this may well be the last show I see the boys in' for fear of getting upset.

Backstage Bill was entertaining us, but even he seemed to be a lot quieter than of late. I had a chat with Derek, and then Mike. I remember Jimmy walking past me and saying "hello Nottingham girl" and I said "I'm impressed you remembered that", and he remarked how he'd remembered me due to our first chat and discussing the music of 'Badfinger'.

Viv had some family issues and needed to phone home, so we needed to find a phone, and so when the time came to leave backstage so that the boys could get themselves ready for the evening ahead, I remember hugging Mike, Derek and John and thinking "this isn't going to happen anymore is it", and due to this thought couldn't actually say anything more than a squeaky 'Bye' and 'Have a good show'. We walked out of the stage doors to the sound of our own footsteps. Once outside, Viv, very teary eyed said to me "Are you alright" and I just looked at her, shook my head and said "no, not really". Anyhow with phone call made we sourced a café. Our, by this time, pre-show drink refresh was a very quiet affair. Each time I looked at Viv over the table she'd say "aww don't look at me like that, I'm going to cry"....................and then we'd laugh. Giggly girls? Not really, we were just fearful of an outcome. We knew if we did cry at that time, we would've cried and cried so much, it could've possibly open the flood gates and we'd be unable to close them again......so yeh, we just giggled. It was our self-preservation strategy.

The double edged sword at this time was Linda, my fellow Nott's pal, had also recently moved away from the Nottingham area too, and I mean m-o-v-e, if she'd have gone any further she'd have got her feet wet, she'd moved to Devon. It happened relatively quickly, so there didn't appear to be any time to get used to the idea, one moment she was there, and the next, she'd gone. So I was already missing my buddy, after spending most weekends together in some form it felt like a missing piece of the jigsaw.

So it really was a case of 'everything' changing. Rather uncomfortable times.

"Moving to Devon was a huge upheaval in my life, so rural and such a different way of life to what I was used to. I felt isolated. Having finished college I started working for my parents, it was expected, never mind that I had secretarial qualifications and wanted to seek my fortune in London".
…as told by Linda Stewart

The usual scramble once the theatre doors were open just didn't happen. Everyone just walked in, and two minutes before show time, there were empty seats here and there. I was so sad to see this. At the 'Civic Hall' the stage is very low……….not one fan attempted to climb onto it. I don't even remember seeing security? Just the regular theatre ushers. No, on this occasion everyone just sat very respectably, clapped, cheered and sang along. My heart was sinking, I just knew, this would be the last time I'd see the boys in concert. Anyhow the stage lights went up, the crowd cheered and there were the boys. Viv's camera was playing silly devils, so I said to her 'not to worry, I'll take some pics with mine, you can have copies'. I took about three photos, and was quite perturbed to be told by an usher quite bluntly, "you can't take photos". WHAT! I think I can, especially when I'd seen other people taking photos the other side of the theatre, as had he. I was really cross. I waited until he'd moved away, and decided to take just a couple more. He came steaming back over, and snapped really quite nasty "Oi you, I'll remove your camera if you do that again", and a chap behind me said "I'd like to see you try". To this day, I have no idea who that gent was, but I do know the usher walked away and never bothered me again. So 'Thank-you' whoever you were, thank you for standing up for me and allowing me to get some photos of the last time I saw the band perform. I really don't know what the ushers gripe was. Give a girl a break will ya, my heart was breaking at this show.

At the end of the concert the audience left in the manner they had arrived, reasonably quiet for teenagers and very respectably.

Viv and I went to the stage door, there were a few fans there, not many 9 or 10, I vaguely remember a slight argument between some of the fans outside, but couldn't be bothered to focus on it really. My mind was totally distraught at the reality of this being quite possibly, 'the last concert'. Anyhow we stood chatting with some fans we knew and then one by one the boys came to the stage door. It was all very nice. We couldn't hang around too long so when Viv and I realized we had our train to catch and we needed to leave………. OH!!! That has to be to this day one of the hardest things I've ever had to do…….the leaving bit…….the walking away bit……….I was absolutely beside myself. On the outside, I was dignified and calm. Maybe I should've taken up acting!? All the fans hugged, saying things like "Keep in touch". We'd never said that before? We didn't need to, because we 'knew' we'd be seeing each other in the next week, the next month, just soon, so immediately that felt alien. Saying 'Goodbye' to the boys……….oh, even now, it stings to think about it………awwww bless those teenage years. We managed to get hugs from all five. Did they think it would be our last concert too? It felt that way. I hugged Jamie then John, then Bill who said to me, "It'll be alright ya know". Maybe not the complete actress I thought I was? My Dad used to say my eyes were always a give-a-way. Then I hugged Derek and then Mike.

Just allow me to say…. to anyone reading this who may be thinking, 'bit over the top'. For one moment, think about your own life, from the ages of 13-17. This isn't like being 21-25., or 36-

40…these four years are of such massive change, mentally and physically. Dare I say quite possibly for girls more than boys. I felt as if my whole life style was slipping away from me. I'd ate and slept this life for almost four years.

Saying goodbye to the boys was very emotional and poignant. I remember 'recording' the last hugs in my mind. I replayed it a lot in the coming weeks, months. Yeh, not many laughs around that time. Christmas came and went and at the beginning of '79 new opportunities had surfaced for me, so I didn't sit twiddling my thumbs by any means. But it was all quite scary, everything had changed beyond recognition.

While I never saw the boys in concert again, Viv and I did do a few more Dagenham pilgrimages in '79, on each occasion we only got to see one boy on each trip. Maybe it was nature's way of getting us off the addiction. There were less girls plodding about the streets on the hunt for the boy's which was a good thing, and a bad thing. We had more one to one times, but we also knew what that stark reality also meant. The last time I saw Derek, he came out of his back gate, stood chatting to us for around an hour, and of course it was lovely and so kind, there we were, just the three of us, Viv, Derek and myself. Then his Mum called him in for dinner. He gave Viv and I hugs, kisses………got to the gate then came back, gave me another hug and said "Be safe travelling home", and with that went indoors……….and that was that. End of a very giddy era. I didn't want to go home I wanted to permanently camp out on the grass verge outside of his house…..forever. As we walked away, Viv put her arm around my shoulders and said "Owww, forra moment there I thought ya wa gonna cry"………….and guess what……….

During 1979 our worst fears were confirmed, and the band was indeed no more. And as the old saying goes, 'It was good while it lasted'. Good? It was fantastic, and we had one hell of a ride up to then didn't we girls.

When the news broke that the band had indeed finished. Ouch………Even though it was expected, it was still horrid to hear…………………………………….I whimpered on and off all day……….it wore me out. In the evening my Mum lifted 'the phone ban', and allowed me to wallow a while in my misery by phoning friends and sharing tears and comforting chats over the phone.

Being honest and without fear of being mocked, for a time I kinda denied the dissolve of the band. For a time after I ached, with that whole 'lack of'…the concerts, the meets, the FANS, yes the lovely fans, those girls that just understood why my brain was working the way it was. I remember my pal Lou referring to it as "well, this must be what it feels like to be dumped"! While quite a harsh statement, I understood where she was coming from. I would shut myself away in my bedroom playing all the records. I couldn't bring myself to read the diaries, still too raw for that. I even went through a 'be it' short period of writing poetry about the band. Yes, poets nationwide waxed lyrical about it back in the 70's…….well…………………maybe not……….but my Mum phoned my Auntie Joyce and said "Oww our Shelley's written some right nice poems", so that was as good as. But I'd be listening to the music while looking at photos, and writing to my friends. Many of whom were going through the exact same withdrawal symptoms. To my mind it was like a strange bereavement. If that sounds extreme, so be it. That's how it felt. Viv came down from Sheffield most weekends to stay at mine, so that made things a little easier for both of us. So I ask again, does it sound a bit over the top? Well imagine yourself travelling somewhere every weekend, meeting up with friends, enjoying a certain type of music, and meeting up with the people who made that music, not to mention spending most of the week leading up to 'that' making plans and chatting to your friends on the phone. Not a few days or weeks of this……but years. Now think, how would you have felt if this had suddenly been taken away from you? This had been part of 'me' almost a quarter of my young life. Those teenage feelings at that time were honest and true. Now being a fully paid up member of adult hood (note – not a grown up, let's not confuse matters!) I understand my teenage self much better now than I did then. It was just one of the many 'first' happenings. It was followed with first job, first show, first boyfriend, first bank account, first drink! Hic!

Yes, very bleak when it ended. I did all the things I needed to, but as in the beginning when so many odd words, gestures, songs, would've fired me up with excitement regarding the boys……..Now those same quips were sending me into a spiral of misery. There wasn't the 'help' that is offered to teenagers now, no helpline, no 'app', no hour special on BBC4……..Nothing. The closest we had was probably the 'Cathy and Claire' page in 'Jackie' magazine, but at that age, right on the cusp of flying into the big wide world and full blown adulthood, my theory on that was, "They don't 'know' me, so how could they possibly understand what I was going through". Even 'I' didn't really understand what I was going through! I knew it hurt. I knew it made me sad. I tried to move on, really I did. I didn't have a boring life, quite the opposite, there was always something going on. It was just hard.

When we were 'in' the exciting times, and at that age, you think "this is going to last forever". Then it all goes as quickly as it arrived. When that happens because you've been on a high for such a long time, in our case years, it is such a drastic empty feeling. At the time you think, you're never going to feel happy again, but, you do………………you do.

A few months later, having been given a part in a local show, I was learning a song at home and for some reason something tickled me during this and I started laughing. I immediately searched out Mum, and said "Mum, I feel a bit guilty, I've just been giggling at this (waving the music in front of her) and I

suddenly realized I haven't thought about Flintlock today, and I feel awful" and instantly got upset, panic!!!.
She said, "Now then, you haven't forgotten about them have you, because you've just mentioned them to me. Secondly, life carries on duckie. I'm sure the boys are all busy and happy individually with whatever they are up to now, and I'm sure they'd want you to be". The lady of course talked sense. She really was the 'best'est friend' I could've had, especially around that time. She just understood, and while she didn't pander to me, she was constructive with support. From then on life did indeed turn around. Not overnight, but it did happen, sooner than I thought it might. My life changed work wise, I was doing more and more singing, I did my first pantomime ('Oh yes I did'………come on, keep up!), and a strawberry blonde boyfriend arrived on the scene, ding dong! In all that time since then, every now and again, the subject of 'Flintlock' would be raised. Either by a friend, family member, or there would be something on TV in a nostalgic program that the boys would be linked with. I'd do a 'smiley sigh' remembering my extremely happy days, and I can say with hand on heart, I don't regret one second of that time back then. It wasn't wasted time by any means. It opened my eyes to different aspects of life, and gave me fabulous experiences. That interest allowed me the luxury of travelling all over the country. And more importantly gave me some wonderful friendships. I've asked myself a few times would I do it all again if I could go back in time? YES, of course, ha ha. I've never lost those warm feelings for the memories and those days, but until very recently I hadn't looked at the diaries and notepads, scrap book and badges, oh and 'the' hat. They'd been put away in a box, for safe keeping and old time's sake, where they still have a secure existence.
Over time when random opinionated people have turned their noses up at my teen-band worship days, I've never bothered to defend my past, why should I? People………….. Never apologise for

having had a fabulous time. To be honest the few that have turned their noses up doth protest too much in a vain attempt to appear 'cool'. I have news, 'cool' people don't need to attempt, they just are.

When I hear of bands making the news these days due to a member leaving or indeed a band splitting up, I can easily sympathise with the fans. My flinty-friends and I feel so lucky, not only did we get to know the boys on a real basis and not just what the media allowed us to know, 'they' also got to know us a little too at the time. Not just faces in a crowd worshiping them from afar. They actually knew of our existence, knew our names, yeh we were lucky.

I decided to look up the word 'Fan' in the dictionary.
'A DEVOTEE OR ENTHUSIASTIC FOLLOWER OF SOME SPORT, OR HOBBY OR PUBLIC FAVOURITE. 'FAN-CLUB' A GROUP UNITED BY DEVOTION TO A CELEBRITY'
....................Not to be confused with the word 'Fanatic'!
That ladies and gentlemen is a whole different thing.

"Probably the last concert I went to was the Wimbledon Theatre one. I screamed a lot, to no avail. I'm sure Bill didn't notice. I got hysterical and carried out by a steward bouncer type for some air....I came back in after a short while and decided to dance instead"
...as told by Lorraine Vickers

"It was the last Gravesend gig which I think may have been their last gig. Jimmy had taken over lead vocals and I think we knew it was the end of an era although we carried on going to Dagenham until early 1979 just to catch the boys".
...as told by Ann French and June Sims

"Gravesend was the last gig - I think we all knew there wouldn't be another after that one. However a lot of us still visited our second home Dagenham for a long time after".
…as told by Helen Morris

"Surbiton Assembly Rooms 1979. I had moved to Devon and persuaded a new friend to go with me. The journey wasn't as easy (and still isn't) as it was from Nottingham, so I knew I was unlikely to make as many trips but then they broke up anyway"!
…as told by Linda Stewart

"I remember clearly the last time I saw them….I knew deep down in my heart that in 1978 at that Gravesend concert when Derek sang so little that this was the end. A very dramatic time for me, it's so weird that here I am at the tender age of 50'something, feeling that passion of my teenage heart".
…as told by Pauline Vincent

So much has happened to everyone since we all parted company in the late 70's….but our feelings and thoughts of those times remain pretty much the same. Linda and I have been friends since that 'meet' on Battersea Park. I sadly lost touch with Viv as we approached age 20, but thankfully after a long search found her again in 2016, which I just can't describe how happy it made me. Lynne and I have had continued contact and meet up's over the years. I was Lynne's bridesmaid, and her lovely daughter Aimee, then 10 years old, was a bridesmaid when I got married. Flintlock sure started something, talk about the ripple effect. I was still kept in the loop of what the girls from the Wimbledon Gang were up to via Lynne, and then years later, many of us met up on face book, and it was so easy, just as though we'd been chatting the week before.

So now my very first pen-pal and long-time friend Lynne gets to have her say.

"I remember waking up one Saturday morning excited about the 'Saturday Scene Roadshow' at the Wimbledon Theatre. Within my circle of friends 'my besties,' I remember someone had made a cake from all of us for either 'Slik' or 'Kenny'!!! Well, they never got it as our attention was quickly diverted away that afternoon by another band called 'Flintlock' who were more our age. From that afternoon it's a bit of a blur, the years that followed were totally dedicated to the fantastic times we all had traveling around the country to see Mike, Derek, John, Jamie and Bill.....sing, play, sign autographs, or just appear! Finding new friends was such a major part of all this. One in particular, Shelley James, became my bridesmaid and God Mother to my daughter.
My Mum and Dad were quite strict so visits to Dagenham on a Sunday afternoon didn't happen often for me. I cringe when I remember my Dad chasing me up the road for getting home late after a great concert at Hampton Wick (no mobiles back then see) it took forever to get home, but it was worth it.
From the big concerts like the New Vic to standing for hours outside Thames TV in what seemed like endless summers, to the amazing more recent meet up's these times were and are special and so unique.

......Lynne (the one with the blue scarf that said she loved Mike) and was convinced she was going to marry him one day!!! Yes, really"!!!
...Lynne Norton - 2016

Here are more thoughts from the girls of how they remember their heady days of youth.

Lorraine Vickers-Bennett... "*A time of great friendship with like-minded females. As it should be, no bitching, no fighting, just a lot of screaming!*"

Fran Norton... "*...and by God, did we scream.*"

Linda White... "*Excited, so full of expectations, waiting for our red rover bus..........and any bus that would get us to Green Lane, ha.*"

Gill Marrion... "*I look back on these days with happy memories. It was the friends that made those years so special. We probably spent 90% of that time travelling, waiting around, queuing, chatting, writing letters, listening to records and making plans. That created a sound foundation for long lasting friendships.*"

Lynne Brown... "*Fun, excitement, carefree, just the best time ever.*"

June Sims... "*A Wonderful way to spend part of our teenage years. We travelled the country, met loads of lovely friends. I always think that it saved a lot of teenage heartache too, as we were too involved with the band to have boyfriends.*"

Ann French… "Spending just over three years of my life travelling the country with my bestie June, making so many friends who we're still in contact with thanks to Face Book. Feeling quite liberated in comparison to school friends because we were 'doing something' every week. It might've been a gig or PA or it might just've been hanging out in Dagenham, chatting waiting around for hours to see the boys. They really were happy carefree days thanks to five boys from Dagenham who we absolutely adored and nearly 40 years later we still hold a special place in our slightly more mature hearts for them."

Jane Davies… "Young and carefree."

Linda Stewart… "Flintlock days were happy, carefree and exciting. They were an introduction to a love of live gigs and a lifelong friend in Shelley. Following the guys meant I went to places I wouldn't have otherwise visited and hung out with a lot of lovely girls who shared the same passion."

Grace Hargreaves… "Happy Days."

Julyet Harris… "To be honest I don't remember a lot of that time in detail. I know it entailed travelling most weekends, lots of gigs, lots of waiting outside various places in all sorts of weathers and long hot summers waiting for the lads to come out of rehearsals for Pauline's Quirkes. I think my parents deserved shares in London transport for the money they gave me to get out and about!"

Helen Morris… *"Being quite a shy person, the boys gave me something in common with so many other girls. Something we could all relate to and share our feelings together. They filled my days, nights, dreams and allowed me to gain confidence and independence. The love and friendship with so many friends made along the way, and kept for many years later. The chance to travel all over the country and almost to Japan! But most of all the ongoing friendships that I still have to this day and all the wonderful memories that I will carry forever. Thanks boys for giving us all the chance to meet."* x

Carole Garratt… *"Exciting wonderful and carefree, just the best times. I met lots of fabulous people, happy days."*

Pauline Vincent… *"For me, it helped me get through a childhood from hell. It was just heaven to me. My god the lies I told so I could see the guys. I did get caught a few times and was badly punished but I don't regret a thing.*
In 1978 when I was 16 I saw the guys for the last time at Gravesend.
It broke my heart that Derek was no longer singing and I knew it would be the last time I saw them. Shortly after that I left home. But the memories of me being wild and care free and the friendships and not forgetting the words to 'Carry Me' will be forever in my heart."

Fran Norton… *"Young carefree days when the only worry we had was whether the boys would be in or not, great friendships formed that have lasted the test of time, some re-discovered via the power of face book and others through the thick and thin of life, sharing the good and the bad together. I will always be grateful for the lifelong friendship that I found with Helen Morris. We danced at each other's weddings, watched children born, a painful divorce and serious heath worries. We may not have lived in each other's pockets but we have always been there for each other when it mattered, and that was all thanks to five young boys from Dagenham."*

I never stopped being a fan of the band………………….
………………………………….The band just stopped being Flintlock.

Remembering Jimmy Edwards
1949 - 2015

Chapter Thirteen… Well FAN-cy That.

After the band split, the fans seemed to scatter in different directions. It's called 'life' isn't it. Some of my 'pen-pals' just stopped writing, and some carried on, regarding those friends the biggest changes were people getting married and having families. Lynne and I were still in touch by letters/phone. In the latter part of '79, I went down to Surrey to stay with Lynne. It felt odd at first in that this would be the first time ever since we met I wasn't going to stay at hers to see the boys. Would it work? Would we have anything in common? I spent two nights at her home, and you know something, we had a great time. We spent some time with a few of Lynne's friends, did some 'girlie shopping', and went to a nightclub. We had such a nice time. I will always remember walking back from our night out, and as we got to Lynne's road, she turned and said to me "Shelley, you know what this means don't you", and I said "What"? She said "the past three days we've spent together, it means we don't need Flintlock to be friends", and she was right. It seemed a sad statement and yet positive at the same time. From then on the friendship has continued to this day.

In 1981 I was out in town one day when I saw a poster outside the Theatre Royal in Nottingham, advertising a show. I stopped dead in my tracks, it was like a musical variety show and whose face and name did I spot on the poster? None other than Michael of Holoway! The last time I'd seen Mike was at my last Flintlock concert in 1978 at Bedford, so it was good to see he'd continued to tread the boards. I popped to the box office and enquired about tickets and decided to get two there and then. I asked my friend Sandra if she'd like to come to the show with me. In past conversations when I'd spoken about Flintlock she'd shown an interest, she said she'd always liked them when she saw them on the TV etc, so she seemed the obvious theatre companion. Indeed she did said yes to the ticket offer, and a few weeks later our theatre outing had arrived. It was a Sunday evening show, and so we decided that we would make a day of it! Our plan was go to the 'Tavern in the Town' (opposite the theatre) for a couple of drinks lunchtime, then have a walk around the arboretum in the afternoon followed by a meal before the show. Apart from hunt down his agent, something I would've done in the past. I had no idea how to contact Mike, so basically I didn't, it was strange, but in the back of my mind I knew I'd see him to talk to. Anyhow Sandra was quite excited at the prospect of seeing Mike for the first time, and so on that basis I'd decided just before the show I'd try and get a message to him so that we could meet up with him afterwards. So my plan was just before the show I'd nip to the stage door with a note. We arrived at the Tavern midday, and I decided to have a bit of fun with Sandra. We got our drinks from the bar and sat in a seated alcove area near the door, she had her back to the door and each time it opened I said "Oh my goodness, it's Mike".......she would freak out and then, of course look around and he wasn't there. I did this several times, each time I made it more and more convincing, and each time she fell for it. As it reached 1pm, the door opened and four men walked in, I just had this feeling they were musicians, and following them I recognized a familiar face. "Oh, Sandra", I said "Mike....he's, he's just walked in".......as I said it the four men were followed in by Mike and Newton!..........Yes, even I was shocked. Sandra was chatting away, so I said again "Er, seriously, Mike's just walked in".......and she just sat there saying "Yeh of course he has" I said "No, really he has" and as I stood up, Mike looked over at me really quite surprised and said "Hey, hello you" and walked over to me for a hug, Newton walked over too and said "Oh of course this is your home town isn't it, long time no see"..........Sandra just looked and wailed "arrrk arrrrkk, arrrrrkkk" and became a jibbering wreck, and stammered out "Ow ow ow ow, helloooooo, I, I, I can't believe this, I thought Shelley was joking". She then asked how we'd arranged it. Mike confirmed, "We didn't arrange it, even I can't believe it"? Talk about right time, right place. It was a lovely surprise. We spent just under an hour chatting to Mike, Newton and the band, catching up and I was asking about the show etc. Sandra and I continued to have a lovely day following on from this, with the sun shining the weather couldn't have been kinder, and later on in the evening after our meal there we were front row of the dress circle watching the show. It took me back to a relatively short period in time. The show was really very good, having spent a little time with Mike, Newton and the band previous it made it all the more special. Mike dedicated a song to me which was sweet. There was no screaming, or shouting, I just waved graciously with the sort of dignity the Queen would've approved of. Afterwards we met Mike and Newton in the bar. From then on, if I was able, I'd go and support him in various shows. 'Joseph and the Amazing Technicolor Dreamcoat' and 'Robin Prince Of Sherwood' were two of my favourites. Such a crying shame 'that' show didn't make it big. Mike's portrayal of 'Robin' at the side of writer/performer Peter Howarth's 'Sheriff of Nottingham' was, in my humble opinion top notch musical theatre and deserved so much more. By the time of 'Robin' touring I was living and working on the east coast of England, but I did venture back to Nottingham for one of the 'Robin' performances at the Theatre Royal, seemed rude not to, Nottingham, Robin Hood, I mean, it had to be done. Just fabulous (*sings* ….'Call me Robin Hood'……….)…and I'll never forget as I sat on the front row (old habits!!) Peter Howarth poised right on the edge of the stage directly in front of me singing 'I'm the Sheriff of Nottingham', and putting the fear of God into me! Wow, he can sing and act a bit can Peter, superb. As it happens I saw that show four times, by the fourth time Mike had left his role as Robin however, and moved onto other productions.

So, yes, I did try to pop along to see show's he was involved with, however it wasn't always that easy, as I was also now on the showbiz band wagon and home had become wherever the work took me, as in Europe and the U.K.

There was one occasion where my friend Caroline and I went to London for the weekend. We'd booked to see a couple of shows, well, if you're in London, you have to go to the West End now don't you. One of our bookings was 'The Pirates of Penzance' at The Theatre Royal on Drury Lane. I'd always wanted to see this show and the bonus was I knew Mike was in this and thought it would be a good chance to have a little catch- up with him. We did indeed see the show, with a host of famous names donning the stage too, Oliver Tobias and Peter Noone to name but two, it was a very glamorous affair, my swash had never been so buckled…….wow, fantastic production. Ironically people of the previous generation in the past during the 'flinty' days had said how Derek reminded them of Peter Noone! Anyhow I'd left word at the Stage Door that we were there, and Mike came to meet us afterwards. We stood chatting and he was saying how the show had swallowed up his life at that time, explaining how he had no free time. He seemed to be aiming this conversation at Caroline, and he said "You see the thing is, when you're in this business you hardly ever get time to see your friends" and Caroline said "You don't have to tell me – looking at me – I never b…..y see her". My straight talking pal, it really was quite comical. She spoke the truth however. My work had also taken over my life, I did try and enjoy 'work free' time though and also saw Mike in a show the week of my 21st birthday. A well'a well'a well'a hu, tell me more, tell me more…….OK, I will…..He was playing the part of Danny in 'Grease' at the Hull, New Theatre (its ok, I didn't bother to jump up onto the stage this time!). My giggly friend Sandra and I ventured to Hull, via York, to eat, drink, celebrate and take in a show or three in the same break. Whenever I did get free time I used it very seriously having fun. Our guesthouse was just across the road from the fire station....so there we were all dressed up with somewhere to go (the theatre, you gathered that bit yeh?) and being as it was a very short walking distance to the theatre off we went, nice summers evening. Now to walk past the fire station it was a good hundred yards (ohh yards, remember them!) we were right in the 'middle of our walk-by' when the siren alarm went off. Well!!! Let me tell you, if you've ever seen a Tom and Jerry cartoon.........that was us. We literally jumped up into the air and bounced off each other, only to look around at some rather naughty firemen, all standing there laughing. Yeh, yeh, very funny lads......we arrived at the theatre looking rather unkempt and flush! It's a good thing that audiences are in relative darkness. We enjoyed the 'feel good' show, and along with the rest of the audience sang and cheered our way through the two hour classic. Afterwards we were treated to nice social time with Mike and a few of the cast.

A rather strange memory I have is being sick at home in the 80's, so there I was flat out on the sofa and watching the Eurovision Song Contest....yes, I was that ill!!! The camera's panned over the audience and guess who I spotted? None other than Newton Wills sitting there in his best bib and tucker! After the 'Flintlock days', for some of the girls there were also a few surprise meet up's with the boys, like these for example.

"I remember bumping into Jamie up town just by chance and very briefly".
...as told by Fran Norton

"Saw Mike and the cast of 'Joseph' in McDonalds in Brum, it was just a chance meeting about 1986".
...as told by Grace Hargreaves

"June and me carried on going to Dagenham until about February '79, mainly popping round to see Bill and Derek on our way home from work".
…as told by Ann French

"I saw Derek at Roots Hall Market in Southend. I can't remember exactly when it was though. I just remember being really happy because he recognized me first. He was helping on a stall and he said 'Hello June', I was shocked. We spoke for a couple of minutes then I had to go".
…as told by June Sims

"Sadly after the Gravesend concert I went to Dagenham once more around Derek's birthday in '78, sniff, sniff".
…as told by Pauline Vincent

"When Terry Gurnhill started driving (17 or 18) she took me, Gill, Julie, Lynne and Lisa up to Dagenham to call on the boys. We were dressed up to the nines and told them we were going to a party. We wasn't! We just wanted to strut our stuff. Think it was John and Bill who wanted to come with us….bit difficult as it was a fictitious party".
…as told by Lorraine Vickers-Bennett

So did those fabulous years of 'Flint'-following leave us all scarred and disturbed? Er, let me have a little think…….NO! Here we all are still talking about those fan-tasticly free and exciting days, as if they happened yesterday. Many of us kept our records, autographs, our many photos, badges and memorabilia. I'd advise any girl, or boy for that matter, to scream at a band!

Apart from having to purchase the odd throat lozenge, it never hurt us.

Some of the girls 'off spring' went onto follow in their mothers fan-worship footsteps…………or did they?

"Well my girls were into Blazing Squad. They used to go to Highams Park and knock at their houses…… what could I say"!
…as told by Fran Norton

"My girls were into 'Blue', took them to meet them at a record shop - that bought back some memories! (the girls were only about 9 and 11 then). Took them to a couple of gigs but they never got addicted to anyone in their teens like we were".
…as told by Ann French

"My daughter had no interest in bands, but my youngest son and I have always gone to gigs together as we share the same tastes".
…as told by Julyet Harris

"My daughter Sarah followed JLS. She and her friend Jenny entered competitions, met them at Radio Clyde, they even went to a number of gigs on one tour on their own, Aberdeen, Glasgow, Sheffield, London, Manchester. I was delighted, as she was doing what I had done and more. Terrific memories for her and me".
…as told by Lynne Brown

"I don't have a daughter, but I have two wonderful sons who not only support their Mum with her

addiction to musical memories, but like going to or playing at real gigs too. Dean, my eldest, is really into punk type bands (and I worried about him when he was in his late teens - I still worry now, will I ever stop worrying). Never used to sleep if either lad was out somewhere late and prayed they would be safe. Glad to say both Dean and Chris are sensible like me!!? And try to steer clear of trouble while enjoying their music. Chris, my youngest, has such a varied love of music and plays various instruments, including Ukelele and guitar quite well. He often puts on one of our 50's, or 60's CD's and sings along".
...as told by Helen Morris

"My daughter just has to put up with her 50 something Mum who is still into following bands around. I have to say over the years I have seen very little trouble at gigs, no fights or drugs. Things like that seem to happen more in nightclubs. I'll stick with the gigs".
...as told by Alison Grey

"My daughter Laura was (and still is) a 'Blue' fan. She didn't have the freedom that I had when I was 13, but we used to go to the concerts together. She reminds me of myself in as much as she loves music and live gigs".
...as told by Gill Marrion

"When my Emma was 11, she was a huge fan of 'Take That'. I told her we were going to a 'Mother and Daughter Beauty Night' in Wembley. We stood waiting for our coach in Eltham and saw many coaches picking up for 'Take That' (big notice on

window screen). When our coach arrived I said to Emma "I'm just going to ask this driver if he knows when our coach is due". I then got on the steps, turned around and shouted to her "are ya coming on then? 'cos I'm going on here" Oh bless her heart, she screamed and cried her eyes out. She and I since then and to this day have seen 'Take That' so many times. But she's never done the silly things I got up to back in my Flintlock days. Emma is now in her 30's, how the heck did that happen"!!!!!!!!
…as told by Pauline Vincent

In 1985 when the film 'Back To The Future' came out, I watched it at the cinema and then for days after was on a roll of "Oww think how great it would be to be able to go back in time and…. watch as my Mum and Dad got married"!...........and "I'd love to do that first show at junior school again…….." etc………but the most reoccurring 'want' of travelling back in time………was to do the Flintlock-days again.

"I'd love a time machine, so that I could go back, even if it was just for one day, to re-live all that excitement, all those thrills and all that laughter"… I've said this to the girls, more than once since we all got back in touch.

So a question……………….If you could see into the future, would you change anything? I'm sure most of us would. I know for sure I'd never have had that second perm! It wasn't so much Donna Summer as Leo Sayer!

However, there was one lady back in the 70's if she could've seen into the future, I'm sure, not only would she have left it exactly as it turned out, but she would never have believed it, I know this for a fact because I've seen first-hand how happy she is. You see for one of the flinty fans, her dream did come true and she did marry one of the boys!

Yes for Teresa Spiteri, the magic did happen and she became Mrs. John Summerton. Teresa had her first proper date with John during the bands diminishing days. Prior to this during those 'Flintlock' years, she too had posters of him covering the walls of her bedroom. And yes, just like the rest of us hormonal teens she had also done the screaming bit, the waiting endlessly to get a look at them bit, the repetitive playing of the records bit. Who says dreams don't come true. How fabulous is that. Hollywood blockbuster perhaps?

David Cassidy and Derek Pascoe……….see, all you had to do was ask! ☺

Teresa and John married on 10th July 1982, and set up home together in their native Essex, they went on to have two children and lived happily ever after.

I actually feel like bursting into song!

………………….…and in Teresa's own words…

"I was mad about John. I had his pictures on my bedroom wall and on my desk lid at school. When I bumped into school friends years later and they realized I'd married John they were like 'No way! But you were mad about him'!!! My best friend that I'd been friends with since the infants, lived opposite John's house back in the '70s. I used to watch out of her window for him all the time. He walked home from school with us once. I seem to think he was with Mike at the time. I was mortified as I was in my school convent uniform, white socks and flat shoes, very attractive, ha ha. After the band split up, for a while I had another boyfriend, but then on a chance meeting John asked me out and that was it, I fell head over heels for him. We got married 10th July

1982. We've always lived in Essex, and John has continued to work in the music industry".

What a wonderful modern day fairy tale…………………

"The best girl won him though. I'm content just being friends. Look after him Teresa" love Helen Morris….xx

Now that is the testament, didn't I say that the Flintlock fans were some of the nicest people I'd ever met.

Chapter Fourteen... Songs, Trails and Puppy Dog Tales.

So, fast forwards to the here and now. Remember 'My Space'? What space? Yeh, that space! Well one of our 'gang' Lorraine Big-Bird-Vickers-Bennett was browsing the interweb and came across the name John Summerton with his very own............'space'. "That name rings a bell" she thought. Come on let's be honest, it must've rang a great whopping bell the size of the O2, and on finding this treasure she informed all of us 'girls'. It was also during this time we were now regular residents of Facebook. Not only did we all get in touch with John via this site also, we gradually all linked up together like a multi-coloured daisy chain, it was exciting, comforting even, with plenty of awwww value mixed in. That became our 21st century meeting place, and we flooded it with photos from our 'fan' times and many memories were shared. On rediscovering each other's lives it was amazing to find out our friends from the past were not only Mummy's now but in some cases Grandmothers! But we were still puppies, how had this happened? And talking of puppy dogs, we discovered John had his own band called 'Beagles', and these guys along with himself all featured on the book of face.

Much to our disappointment we'd also discovered that there had indeed been a little Flintlock reunion a few years previous that none of our circle had been aware of.........Took us weeks/months to come to terms with that bit of news I can tell ya!

Due to the discovery of John and the Beagles in the year 2010 the girls decided to get together at a venue in Essex called 'The Lodge'. The reason for this particular venue being chosen was 'Beagles' were playing there, and so the girls organized their own little reunion. Due to work commitments I couldn't attend. It was lovely to see all the photos that followed the event on face book afterwards though. John had even managed to get Bill along to see the girls again, and so it made it extra special for them.

Here are some of the memories from the girls that did go.

"Ann and I went to see John at the studio on the day we all met up at The Lodge. She was so nervous even though she'd spoken to him on the phone. When we went in he made us a cup of tea and was as nervous as we were. The night at The Lodge was surreal. It was amazing to catch up with some old friends and make some new ones".
…as told by June Sims

"I remember when I was talking to him on the phone I was thinking 'this is John Summerton and he phoned me"! Since then we've had some great nights watching the Beagles and some after show laughs in The Lodge hotel rooms. It was great when they played at June's wedding too. Meeting Teresa was a breath of fresh air because she's 'one of us', a lovely lady".
…as told by Ann French

"Regarding The Lodge, I can't remember how I found out, but it was fantastic meeting up with the old gang and John and Bill being there, so much catching up to be done and meeting the lovely Teresa. I remember being so glad that she was a nice person and they so obviously adored each other. The night was finished off with John and Teresa joining us for a night cap in the room, it was truly a great evening filled with fun and laughter".
…as told by Fran Norton

"I had found out that John was involved with the Beagles via YouTube footage. I have seen them perform three times, all thanks to Ann and June for

organizing the meet-ups. Great to meet up with John again, great voice as well as guitarist. Bill showed up at The Lodge to play keyboard, he had not changed a bit. The rest of the band (Beagles) were great, just took us all under their wings, or should that be paws"?
...as told by Lynne Brown

"It was Ann or June that contacted me to let me know about The Lodge, and after agreeing to go along with Fran my knees began to tremble followed by a couple of weeks of really bad nerves. How I managed to drive down to Essex I'll never know, and I nearly turned back. Met all the old gang in the afternoon and of course we all shared photos and catch-up gossip. It was like we had never all been apart. Couldn't believe John recognized us after all these years and he introduced us to Teresa who became one of the gang immediately, they are such a lovely couple. Beagles played that night and we had such fun. It was my 50th birthday a few days after and so they sang Happy Birthday, which was lovely, but me still being shy got typically embarrassed. The after gig get together was great too, apart from the sandwich tray"!
...as told by Helen Morris

Disappointed I couldn't go to The Lodge for that reunion?……..just a smidge. I think the days that led up to it, and even a few following it of me blurting out every five minutes, 'ARRKKKKK I CANT BELIEVE I CANT GO TO THE REUNION', would've been a slight hint to anyone within a 50 meter radius. But I had to put the work contracts first, oh the joys of being self-employed. You can't pull a sickie when you're on lead vocal.

Fortunately later on in the year, Ann told me there was to be another get together, Friday 5th November. I couldn't believe it, not only did I have a gig penciled in on the work calendar I also had teaching that afternoon. Grrrrr, and cries of "ARRRRKKKK I CAN'T BELIEVE………" etc started up again, I was gradually turning into Victor Meldrew! However, the fortune fairy did sprinkle some magic dust around just a couple of weeks later. Not only had the gig for that particular date been pulled, it had been moved to a later date. Ahhhh, I could actually hear my accountant breathing a sigh of relief.

So I just needed to ask my '521 Singers' if I could change their teaching date. This is a group of people I teach singing, that are of the 'older, more mature generation'. I explained to them why I was desperately wanting to change the date……Flinty-girls, Flintlock, John, Beagles, bla bla bla………I thought 'just be honest Shelley'. And in reply they went into the whys and wherefores of why Pat Boone and Tommy Steel had had a similar effect on them…………and that was only the men! Joking aside, the ladies were very sympathetic and cackled protectively around me like little hens. The men however just sat looking at me with rather blank expressions. The upside was the ladies had the final say. Don't we always! So a class for the following week was arranged…….and so their rousing renditions of 'Busy Doing Nothing' and 'I Can't Get No Satisfaction' didn't suffer too much. (No pensioners were harmed in the re-arranging of this lesson.)

As this was all planned a few days before hand, and Essex isn't around the corner from north Nottinghamshire, there was still a concern we wouldn't be able to go. 'We' being me……..and him indoors……. the husband also a musician. Yes………….even I took the plunge, which is silly really 'cos I just fancied the idea of having a boyfriend. It didn't happen until my late 30's though. Far too busy for all that mortgage and choosing curtains lark before then. I met Alan in Southport, I said "Flippin' eck fancy seeing you here"……..and that was a joke!...... I'd been offered a job there as singer with a band, and he was also in the band as guitarist. We hit it off right away, mainly by making each other laugh! He asked me to marry him after the lengthy courtship of five weeks! I still think it was a dare, back-fired then didn't it! Friday arrived, as they tend to do at the end of a week, and it was looking like, yes indeed we would be travelling down to Essex. As we hadn't been able to say in concrete that we 'could' go, I'd only been in touch with Ann, and not said a word to the other girls about a possible visit. I didn't want to do that whole "yes, can't wait to see you all" only to double back with "sorry, can't make it" routine. Also as Ann lives so close to The Lodge, she was the ideal person to inform me 'if' there was an outside chance the gig wasn't going to happen. Due to a gig of our own the following evening we couldn't stay over like the girls were, they were filling most of the rooms of the Lodge's B&B accommodation.

We hopped into the car and I think we were 30 minutes into the journey when I started with "Are we nearly there yet". (She was a bit giddy). The giddiness was tested to extremes however, when we came up against not one, not two, but three delays due to traffic accidents along the way. The third one of the day sadly being a 7 car pile up which we'd been informed about via the radio travel news, so quick thinking on Alan's part, we exited off the motorway before we got to the point where we couldn't. It was ridiculous. While all this was happening I was texting Ann saying 'another accident, be there as soon as……….', and she was texting back saying, "we're all here now, please be careful' etc. These delays cost us an extra 55 minutes onto the journey, so it had taken us over 4 hours to get there. I get travel sick when we get to the bottom of the road where we live, so this was not ideal. I think the excitement however overtook the travel 'icky feeling, as we pulled into the car park and as if by magic I felt as fresh as a daisy................I've never really known what that means? Have you ever seen a daisy that looks travel sick for example? But, I'm going off the subject, so, there we were, out of the car, walking rapidly across the car park, opening the door of The Lodge, and walked into the bar where all the girls were circled around a cluster of tables. Lorraine was the first one to spot us, although she looked at me as if to say "I feel like I should know her...but..........Oh Oh Oh", her face was a picture, and then gradually the penny dropped. There was the equivalent of a Mexican wave which erupted around the table. Lynne stood up and holding out her hair in a 'Great Scott Marty' kind of fashion said "OH, MY bleep bleep GOOD GOD"....and during the mega hug episode I heard John say "Is that Shelley James strolling in here like royalty". Alan (husband and head coffee maker) said I then disappeared into a gaggle of girls! How awful of me, but I'd forgotten he was even there for the first fifteen minutes. Far too busy giggling, hugging, chatting, we could've been back in 1978! I then realized he of guitar twanging expertise wasn't close by, and Lynne saw me looking for him. "Oh Shelley" she said "sorry, but I've just introduced Alan to John and their now talking about guitars and for me it could be a totally different language so I've left them to it". I looked across the room and sure enough there was Alan talking to John. Now 'that' was freaky! My husband (and that title is still hilarious to my mind as it is) talking to John Summerton, of 'Flintlock'. It was like being in some weird parallel world. I walked over and hugged John, to my mind it was as if I'd seen him a few weeks before. It was such a lovely atmosphere, so easy and friendly and just an absolute joy to be spending time with all those lovely people. To say three decades were between the time we'd all last been together, you wouldn't have known it.

Beagles did their first set and were great. During the interval we were all chatting ten to the dozen and taking photos, many, many photos. During the second band set June came over to me, the music was loud (that wasn't a complaint by the way) and I couldn't catch what she was saying, so she showed me a list of songs and I swear, I thought she said "which one do you like", thinking 'oh she's going to ask the band to do it'. So I pointed to a Beatles classic "Saw Her Standing There". A few songs later John announced "Right, little treat for you now, we have a guest singer, and she's gonna come up here and sing for you, come on Shelley"…………I am a professional singer….honestly…………but EEEeeeeeeeeee! (Thank goodness I didn't choose 'Wandering Star'!)

So exciting………yes…………SO exciting. I'm on the stage, singing, and there is John at the side of me. Can you imagine back in 1978 if anyone had said to me "In 2010 you'll be singing on the same stage as John", I'd have booked them into the nearest hospital. But there I was, singing 'with' John, I just rocked my way through the song and loved, loved, loved it, and as this was happening I looked out onto this audience of lovely friendly faces, yes it was just one of those moments. One of those moments you don't need to write down actually, because it stays with you forever. A few weeks previous to this trot down to Essex I'd actually sang backing vocals to Neil Sedaka's songs, performed in front of 'THE' Neil Sedaka. Now don't get me wrong, it was amazing, very enjoyable, very special, how could it not be. However singing with John and his band was for me, a far bigger buzz.

Ten, possibly fifteen minutes after that I eventually managed to peel myself off the ceiling. When I got back to my seat Lynne said "do you want me to pinch you, oh my God that was like a dream"…"I KNOW" I said. I knew exactly what she meant, it was so surreal.

The gig eventually ended and we'd all had the most fantastic evening. It was midnight and Gill said "I know it's really late and you pair have to travel home, but please come up to the room and have one drink with us all before you go, we haven't seen you in such a long time". Well, I looked at 'himself' and he said "Yes of course, it is a few hours to get home, but I haven't seen Shelley smile this much in ages", and doesn't that make me sound like a grumpy drawers! I'm not by the way. We did stay behind a while and the half an hour turned into three hours, so it was 3am before we eventually left. Totally worth it though, what a smashing evening we'd had. The goodbye hugs and kisses alone took 15 minutes. We eventually landed back home at 5 minutes past 6……..am………A.M!!! I knew there was a 6 o'clock, but since my early 20's figured it was always followed with P.M.

How long would we have to wait before another gathering like that? Not long……the following year to be precise.

So 6th May 2011 we all headed back to The Lodge again. There were a few more of the gang meeting up on this occasion and we got there a little earlier so that we could spend time together in the afternoon too. On arriving and unpacking a few bits and bobs, I ventured to June's room, 5 of us to be exact crammed into that room, drinking coffee, eating biscuits and sitting cross legged on the bed, we could've easily all been in our teens again. Helen had brought some of her Flintlock photos from the 70's, so we were all looking at them with the same interest and chatter we would've done back then. Our reason for choosing this date to meet apart from Beagles playing at The Lodge again, was that 7 of us were having birthdays within 10 days of each other around this date, so it seemed rather apt.

Around 7pm we all made our way downstairs to the bar area where the band were setting up the gear. John and Teresa came over to us, and so hugs all round. When he got to me he said

"Hello Shelley, where's Alan"……………………honestly, I'm used to the concept now, but at that point, my brain couldn't cope! Alan had to make a couple of calls, but then gradually as the bar filled he appeared. Not in a magical illusion way, he just walked down the stairs. Once again a lovely atmosphere as we all greeted each other. We'd previously decided that we would have a little after gig party in one of the rooms and Liz had very kindly made us all the most tasty, beautiful sparkly cupcakes. I mean, they were cakes that sparkled, what's not to like. Before the gig began we were all standing around talking, catching up and generally putting the world to rights, when the door opened and these two men walked in.

You know when you're not expecting someone and then you suddenly see them, so the recognition isn't as instant as it would've been, well that's what happened to me. 'Ohhhhhh where have I seen him before'…….. *ponderment*…….and then it clicked. It was BILL. So never mind that Bill probably wouldn't have remembered me in a million years………these were not normal circumstances, so I just held out my arms and said "Bill, come here I need to hug you"……….and he just walked towards me and held his arms out. (Thought for the day – maybe I should've used this obvious line many years previous, after all, it appeared to work!). John was standing close by and said "Bill, do you remember Shelley? Oh and that's her husband standing there, so you might want to hug him too"….and with that after my hug, Alan got one too. It was very funny and typical Bill. He hadn't changed one bit, still 100% the chap we loved back then. So what gem did I open up with? 'Long time no see Bill'? or 'Hey, great to see you after all these years'?…………Nooooo………without a second thought I found myself saying "Bill, I need to apologise for standing outside your house most Sunday afternoons from 1977 to 1979, I think they call it stalking now". He looked at me, laughed and then said "You haven't been carrying that around with you all this time have you"......"er, to a certain degree" I said. He was with his rather bemused friend Paul, who I was informed was also a musician, and played in a jazz combo with Bill. It was lovely to stand there chatting to the pair of them, and again, so easy. I later found out that evening, that all the girls knew Bill was going to turn up, but wanted it to be a surprise for me, awwww.

During the evening there were a couple of occasions where John called Billy boy up onto the stage to join in with the band, and that was just fabulous to see the pair of them on the same stage again. Let me tell you, the nostalgia vibe this particular evening was overwhelming. A few numbers on from this and John called me up onto the stage to do a reprise of my Beatles number I'd performed with them back in the November. Bill at this point was in the audience and during the song he gave me the thumbs up sign. What a night. I have no idea how John did this, but during the evening he gave every single one of us 'girlies' a mention over the mic. Now that is one heck of a memory, not only all the names but the area's we'd traveled from........'John Summerton – Memory Man'.......new act for you there John.

After the gig it was all back to Fran's as that was the biggest room. We'd all taken nibbles, drinks etc, and we may not be 16 anymore but we certainly know how to party. Toffee vodka having a hand in that....hic! By 4am we were all flagging a bit, ha ha, so we called it a day. The following morning only half of the gang surfaced for breakfast, but we carried on where we'd left off, catching up. Yep, still puppy dogs, old tricks.

In 2012 Lynne had a party for her 50th Birthday and Beagles were going to be the house band that night, augmented for a few numbers by myself and himself. Even though Lynne's birthday is in January she'd had the party late May and it was a lovely balmy summers evening. The party was out in the Surrey countryside in a barn, and as well as lots of the flinty girls I'd seen quite recently there were also some faces I hadn't seen since the 1970's, which was fabulous. It was also lovely to see 'Mum and Dad Tuvey', in fact I stood chatting to them about the first time I stayed at their home back in 1976. I remember Ken (Lynne's Dad) saying "you were so shy back then Shelley, I can't believe you're going to get up there tonight and sing". But I was and I did, and yes.......another of those "Is this really happening" moments. As I stood there singing with John on guitar one side of me, my husband on guitar the other and only the flamin' Wimbledon gang of girls right in front of me dancing the night away, I realized how special this was. What a great evening. However the most obscure bit of that night for me was getting half way through singing the 'Blondie' number 'Call Me' and spying Big-Bird Lorraine, standing on a table in the distance taking photos...............some things never change, and quite honestly, I wouldn't want them to.

Very sadly whilst writing this book, Gary Parish the drummer with 'Beagles' passed away. He was a great muzo and a genuine nice guy, and will be remembered fondly by everyone that knew him.

Chapter Fifteen... Carry On Screaming.

It was the late great Ethel Merman who sang 'There's No Business, Like Show Business', and she was spot on, there isn't. It has to be the most social-anti-social line of work. Don't get me wrong, I've now been in 'The Biz' a little longer than five minutes and I've always felt fortunate my hobby became my job. Some of the experiences I've had due to my career have been wonderful. I have worked in amazing venues, countries, and with some lovely people. More often than I could've dreamed of I've experienced those moments of "Has that just happened, 'I've' just been part of that"? Sometimes you're even lucky enough to meet and work alongside people you've admired for years. By no means is this a name drop moment, when I met these people I was as giddy as a kipper and so being reserved and in control didn't even come in to it. For me, Bob Monkhouse, Gerard Kenny and Victoria Wood come to mind. Victoria even sent me a lovely letter after meeting her. Still waiting on that text from Ms. Streisand however!!! *taps fingers on table*. I love what I do, but it comes at a price. When everyone is out to party then that is most likely the time when you're working. From the other side of the coin in the past I've had to miss birthdays, weddings, even funerals all down to work commitments. When it looks like you've only done an hour, two hours work, and yet it took you 2/3 hours to get to the venue, it will be 2/3 hours to get home, and you did your rehearsing/prep work a few days before hand etc, not to mention the 'hanging around' bit.....well these are all parts of the job the public don't see. You work hard to make it look easy. So as I look back now with years of experience under my belt I totally feel for how hard the boys worked back in the 70's. They had the enthusiasm and energy of youth on their side yes, but even so, they never seemed to stop, and on the rare occasions where they should've been relaxing in their homes, there we were, the fans,

hovering on a regular basis outside their havens……Oops…*side steps away*
In our minds back then we didn't class it as harassment at all, it was a plain fact we just adored them.
There were times when due to the sheer number of fans it wasn't easy for the boys to get from A to B, so here are a few special memories from Flintlocks tour manager.
Over to you Newton!

"The Flintlock fans were very special, always good to arrive at a venue and see people you recognize. How did they manage to travel all over the UK and buy tickets for so many gigs.
I still remember so many fans after all this time. Most of the fans were great, not all! …. And there were a few problem mothers!
I remember one fan, Grace from Birmingham. One gig at the Apollo/Victoria London we were on stage setting up, a voice from nowhere called "Newton", I replied "where are you"? "It's Grace and I'm up here", "where's here"? I called back. Grace was way up in the top of the stage. "How did you get there" I asked, "I went into Woolworths next door, went onto their roof and climbed onto the roof of the theatre and then climbed down here above the stage" she said.
Fans were quite different in each country we visited. In Japan we arrived at Tokyo airport to mayhem. Flintlock were last off the plane. I looked out to see sheets of glass windows moving in the airport as thousands of fans beat on the windows. The airport staff and police just looked on smiling! They hadn't seen anything like it and were not sure what to do. We had to move and quickly. I grabbed a policeman

and asked if there was another way out from the plane. In the end he said there was an underground route underneath the runway. "Let's move"!!! All very James Bond. During that visit Flintlock were due to meet fans at the biggest department store in Tokyo. Our record company collected us in a bus. We hadn't gone far before we came to a stop, a traffic jam. We kept telling the driver to go another route as we were due at the store in five minutes. He shot down some side streets and arrived at the back of the store, only to find out that the jam was caused by Flintlock fans, thousands of them! We climbed through the windows of the bus and onto its roof. From there we were pulled onto the roof of the store. Then when we finally got into the store we were met by 5000 fans!
On the day we were to leave Japan for home the police said we had to leave the hotel at midday. "No way" I said, our plane doesn't leave until 10pm. "We can't guarantee your safety" came back the police "We believe the fans intend to follow you to the airport, you will leave at midday". Midday we left with a dozen police cars leading, lights flashing and another convoy of fans behind being driven by parents or in taxis. The car we were being driven in had the radio tuned into an American radio station playing 50's music, my kind of music. The music suddenly stopped and the announcer had a news report to say that Elvis had died. So when they say 'what were you doing when you heard about the death of Elvis'...........I do remember.
A similar chase was in Dundee, Scotland. I ended up driving the Flintlock car into a 'Mother's Pride'

factory to hide. While it was a lovely smell, you should have seen the faces of the bakers".
.........Newton Wills - 2016 (Flintlock's Tour Manager 1970's)

It's strange isn't it how things often go full circle. With various shows and tours I've done, most of the theatres I screamed at Flintlock in, I've now actually sang in myself. I remember a few years ago, I was at the Towngate Theatre in Basildon, and trotting about backstage with a coffee waiting to do the sound check when I spied some large black and white photographs on the wall. They were of the casts of previous pantomimes they'd produced at the theatre. I moved in closer to look at the 'Jack and the Beanstalk' photo, and there's 'Mike' at the top of the beanstalk......now there's something you can't say every day! Much to the amusement of the people I was appearing at the theatre with, I found myself saying out loud to the photo "Ow hi Mike".........and without trying, my head was suddenly filled with past memories. They seemed like a lifetime ago, and also just yesterday.

I wasn't the only one keeping diaries back in the day, some of the fans like myself also kept written recollections of dates and happenings. Even one of the Flintlock boys felt the need to record events and experiences around that time........so with his kind permission here is a direct lift word for word from John's diary.

May 15th 1976
"Got up at 9.00. Mick picked me and Jamie up in Blue Victor. Got to Orpington at 10.15 went to Pinnacle Records ....then went to first chart return shop....lots of girls about 350 sold 55 singles went back to Pinnacle had something to eat. Lots of girls taking photos. At 1.45 went to Croydon but couldn't find the shop. Then when going down

main road we saw lots of girls about 400 all in the road stopping the traffic. All of the girls were chanting FLINTLOCK RAH RAH RAH. We got into the front of the shop and signed a few autographs, all the girls would not be quiet screaming loud. We went to the back room for an hour, by now Mick had called the police!!! 27 of them and an ambulance, now over 2000 girls.

They were told we had now left and to go home. They were now back in the street and the police couldn't control them. We had to go over the roof through the fire escape and lifts…..really great…..went back to Pinnacle for tea and food, got home at 6.30. Derek came round had a chat, got 4 letters this morning Sheffield, Sunderland and Reading…..also Mum said we got to get phone number changed, when any girls phone up Mum says I've moved."

May 24th 1976.
"Good day at school, round Mick's at 4.30 pull away at 5.00. Newton and Allen in the Mercedes. Got to Nottingham at 8.30, went on at 9.45 off at 10.00. Really quick but good. Lots of girls and Tony Prince really nice bloke, home at 1.30".
(John Summerton)
………..just a regular couple of days then!

When I began to write this trip down a fan-based memory lane I didn't take into account what a journey I would find myself on……..Oh yuk, 'journey', don't you just cringe at all these newfangled quotes……..Thinking outside the box! Bringing it to the table! Going on an emotional journey! And ….. just let me put this past you………..to me, 'thinking outside the box', "do I really want another chocolate when I've just closed the lid"……..'Bringing it to the table', usually means dinners ready. 'Going on an emotional journey', "I'm travelling to a gig, will it be cash pick up or a cheque"…..and 'just let me put this past you'……….."shift"!…….. Anyhow, journey or not, it did stir up emotions. In the early stages of putting together this Fan-biography, I asked my

'Singy-Sister' Fiona to give the first chapter a read. Not so much feedback, as 'Feeb's back', see what I did there! ...On doing so she said even though she didn't recall Flintlock she had empathy for the emotions of the teenage adornment and obsession. She also liked the references to my Mum, and while 'I' knew that the Flintlock memoirs would have me in stitches one moment and tear's the next, after all they were written with my teenage mind set and innocent heart, what I hadn't bargained for was the many references to my dear Mum. Reading all the dairies and notebooks again and reading her input and comments, it was like getting a little piece of her back. I haven't mentioned it as yet, but she had a little speech that would without fail be repeated on quite a regular basis each time a Dagenham visit would occur.

"Have you got a clean hankie? Have you enough money? Don't forget my three rings, remember your manners and be careful."

It would have been far easier for her to have just made a recording. I would leave the house saying "yeh, yeh", and she'd call "never mind yeh, yeh madam". Without her total support and trust, then I wouldn't have had the fabulous teenage experiences I did. I recall these times with such great fondness and affection. Whenever anything fan club related dropped through the letter box I swear she was almost as excited as I was and took a genuine interest in the band. The December of 1976 was no exception post wise. The fan club issued each fan club member with a silver EP floppy disc with each of the boys sending a Christmas message. Woohoo! What a fabulous Christmas treat.
I think Jamie spoke for all of us when he said..........

"Well, the last two years have certainly been the most exciting in my life so far".
............Jamie Stone – 1976

So could there possibly be anyone reading this wondering how the rest of the 'boys' recall those times?
Well, wonder no more............................

"My view of that time is that the fans were the key to success and we were so over worked, particularly me with 'The Tomorrow People' as well, that on reflection I wish we'd had more time to show appreciation of the devoted following myself and the group had.
From the age of 12 - 17 I knew one thing, work like a bugger day in day out. Learn multiple scripts, songs, and gigs by the dozen. It was a crazy time, but great highs as well as the low points that you feel with all that pressure at that age. When punk rock came along we couldn't and were not allowed then to cross over our image and music, and along with my family breaking up at that time I regret that the whole success at this point did not reap the rewards I think should have come our way......that's Show Biz folks.
..........Mike Holoway - 2016

"Being in the band represented a weird and wonderful alien world apart from the normality that had been my childhood up to that point.
At first I was both flattered and incredulous at all the attention, and I was aware of a sense of duty on my part. I felt if someone had taken the trouble to come all the way down to Dagenham then the least I

could do was to take some time to speak with them. This over time changed into real relationships as familiar faces returned and a hierarchy was established between the regular fans, who felt themselves disconnected from the day trippers. Thinking back now the relationship I had with the fans was secondary only to the relationships with the guys in the band and, perhaps just as significant. I would say that over about 4 years there was hardly a day when I did not spend a good part of it on my doorstep talking to the fans.

I grew up under the scrutiny of the fans, and it made for a very exacting upbringing. At times the cutting caustic observations at every detail of my work rest and play could cut to the bone.

I now realize that all of that time spent in their presence was the most important of educations. All of my social skills were acquired on the doorstep talking to this cross section of society from Richmond to Glasgow. We shared a common link that had everything and nothing to do with music.

There are always regrets...but on reflection, they are personal and petty. I now have come to realize that it was a truly unique and amazing slice of life and was an education that is available to a lucky few".

…………..Derek Pascoe - 2016

"To be honest a branded record label would have been nice. Looking back we had so many offers from some of the big players, RAK (Mickey Most), Dick James, Elton John's label and a few others, but saying that we had some good times with everyone at Pinnacle. To be honest, Mike's dad, Mick, did a great *job and who knows maybe the big labels would have wanted to change us too much.*

Those days seem so long ago now. My wife Teresa found a bag of old fan mail last year, and reading them now b......y hell! You fans were serious!!! Nationwide, from Brighton to Inverness and everything in between. And the logistics of planning and funding (bank of Mum and Dad?) all the trips and concerts and PA's you all turned up for, and all without mobile phones.

Personally I never appreciated until now how hard it must have been for you all to get to a gig, normally three hours before the band would arrive. As for us, well it was easy, just jump in a car and wake up in Hull, Liverpool, wherever, sometimes not knowing where I was actually!

............John Summerton - 2016

'Ah, a different world back then. Days when fans could sleep overnight in a Dagenham phone box and still be alive in the morning, and trousers you could park two buses in.

Nowadays fans have it way too easy, our girls were hard-core. They had an intelligence network to rival the CIA and the ability to organize mass gatherings at the drop of a hat. If Saddam Hussein had got his hands on them he'd still be in power. Happy days.........

Happy days.......
..............Bill Rice - 2016

I would have been 8 or 9 years old when during the school Summer holidays my Mum decided we'd go on a hike of about a hundred mile walk (In later years I realized it was less than 2, but at that age going ten miles across the town on a bus felt as if we'd arrived in China). And why would that be? I hear you ask. Well, it was to stand behind a rather high wire fence all afternoon…….yes, wire fence, all afternoon, and that isn't me exaggerating due to my tender age, we literally stood there approximately 4 hours along with the majority of the female 40 something population of Nottingham. I couldn't believe it. My precious Spirograph time was being swallowed up for this! Whatever 'this' was? I leaned on the fence, I bounced against the fence, I pressed my face on the fence in a attempt to look like a waffle, I sat on the grass, I stood up again, and kept repeating the cycle until my Mum piped up "Oh for goodness sake our Shelley stop fidgeting, it won't be long now, just be patient". Patient…..what for? I could tell by the surroundings this wasn't going to end in my favour, I mean I hadn't spotted a single ice cream van all afternoon. The hours passed by and my Mum chatted and laughed with other like-minded women, who also enjoyed spending their afternoons looking through wire fences. Suddenly my opinion of my Mum changed in a matter of minutes. A couple of cars drew into the car park which was protected by said wire fence, and the women went crazy. I was plastered up against that fence protected by Mum behind me, but she wasn't being very 'Mumsy'. She along with all the other ladies began whooping and calling out. I couldn't figure it out, why would she do this just because a car had pulled into the car park? How odd. Then while a couple of people came out of the building connected with the car park, two gentlemen got out of the front of the first car and one opened the door to the back of the car. Gripping stuff eh!? Then another man got out of the back of the car and the women went loopy, including 'my' Mum. The 'man'

casually walked closer to the fence, and the screams and cheers went louder. He waved, and the cheers became louder still. The 'man' walked a little closer towards the hordes of female worshipers and this woman excitedly called out "Kick yer leg up Frankie", but it wasn't just any woman, it was my Mum!!! On hearing this he did indeed 'kick his leg up', and if it was possible the screams and cheering of these women went off the Richter scale. They threw flowers, notes and even panties over the fence to the sophisticated gent. He then blew kisses, called out "I love ya" "hey, thank you" smiled a lot, waved some more and then flanked by the other chaps disappeared into the building, the screams subsided and all the women were crying. Was that it? Really! We'd been there all that time, for no more than 5 minutes of a chap waving! "Not exactly what I'd call a good afternoon out" I can remember thinking. However, on the other hand my lovely Mum was so happy. She had the biggest smile on her face. It was then I realized my Mum wasn't just a Mum or a women, she was 'a girl'. I knew she was in a great mood as on the way home we stopped off at the local corner shop and I was treated to a Sherbet Dip, something I wasn't usually allowed to have. We arrived home and my Mum trotted into the house all smiles like she'd had a couple of sherries. The biggest shock for me was my Dad didn't seem to mind! He actually sat there and asked her about the afternoon, and she then went into this rather different version of events as to how I'd seen it, umm interesting. She was happy, and he, it seemed was glad she was happy. I sat confused. My Dad said to me "You alright Blue? Ya look a bit fed up ma duck". I wasn't fed up, I was just trying to understand why that man in a car park had put my Mum into such a good mood (and was now the time to ask for that Petite Typewriter I'd had my eye on?).
It turns out the 'man in the car park' was
singer/actor/entertainer and all together good sort Frankie

Vaughan, one of my Mum's idols, (the other being Englebert Humperdinck). I learned this over the following evening/days as Frankie's LP's were played to extreme in our house. Not that it was of any use to me back then, but I knew all the words to 'Green Door' before the day had ended.

When I was 19 and totally at one with the whole screaming 'thing' I took my Mum as her birthday treat to the Commodore International in Nottingham to see Frankie in concert. Seeing him through my 19 year old eyes I realized he was this suave and handsome chap. He sang all his hits, told amusing stories and wandered around the tables shaking hands and kissing the ladies. Mum got her very own kiss that evening and was in her element, and I was in mine, because by this time I knew exactly what it meant to her. It's just a safe, exciting and magical little world you can escape to, be it for just a few hours. He gave her the moonlight alright.

Later that same year I was able to take her to see Mr. Humperdinck in concert too, Leicester De Montfort Hall no less.......and she's back in the room! We had row H, I remember this clearly as I was a little disappointed on booking the tickets. Anyhow I don't quite know to this day how she wangled it, but on arriving and plonking ourselves down in our seats Mum then sourced an usher, got chatting to him and the next thing I know he is escorting us down to the front row where we sat quite comfortably to the right hand side (stage left as we call it!!) of the stage for the duration of the show…..thank you very much. Arrh now I see where I get it from.

In 1997 I was lucky enough to work alongside Frankie Vaughan, and what a nice gentleman he was, he had a voice that sounded like velvet with eyes to match.

I have also been very fortunate to do backing vocals for Englebert Humperdinck which took place in the latter part of the 'noughties', what a fantastic production that was. You see as I write this, for the past 10 years I've been associated with doing backing vocals for singer/entertainer Joe Longthorne, and Joe had been asked to perform at a 'Variety Club Presentation' in Manchester in honour of Englebert. Due to this, 'Eng' said he would also like to sing a few songs during the evening, and would it be alright to use 'Joe's band and backing vocalists'...would it? Not 'arf!!!!! The stuff dreams are made of. That moment as he turned on the stage at the end of the show to thank the band, well, it has been forever engraved in my mind. He even gave 'me' a bouquet of red roses after the show! A very handsome and charming man, Mother certainly had good taste. I feel so very fortunate I was invited to be part of these shows. By this time I sadly didn't have my Mum anymore, but I'd like to think she somehow saw those rather special occasions.

So it's been going on for years, and years, and I'm sure will continue to do so. To all those bands that have made millions of hearts flutter in the past, that have made us laugh, cry, worship from near and far. Thank you for the amazing and exciting experiences we've all been allowed to share with you. From The Beatles to The Osmonds, The Bay City Rollers to Duran, Duran, Take That, McFly, etc, in fact every band lucky enough to have been given this very special privilege of unconditional love, thank you. Every generation thinks they are the first to scream at a band, and you know what, that's OK, that's just as it should be, it should feel new, and special and yours.
Yes technology is changing fast and I imagine there will be a time when you blink and you've ordered concert tickets with a thought pattern linked up to a computer chip in your big toe. But will there ever be a time when girls stop screaming at boys?

……………………………..I doubt it.

Thank you 'Flintlock' for carrying some of us a little of the way. x